Breaking Free of the Web

BREAKING FREE OF THE WEB

Catholics and Internet Addiction

KIMBERLY YOUNG, PSY.D.
PATRICE KLAUSING, O.S.F.

ST. ANTHONY MESSENGER PRESS
Cincinnati, Ohio

Cover and book design by Mark Sullivan
Cover photo © www.istockphoto.com/Alex Nikada

LIBRARY OF CONGRESS CATALOGING-IN-PUBLICATION DATA

Young, Kimberly S.
Breaking free of the web : Catholics and internet addiction / Kimberly Young, Patrice Klausing.
p. cm.
Includes bibliographical references and index.
ISBN 978-0-86716-804-4 (pbk. : alk. paper) 1. Internet addicts—Religious life.
2. Internet addiction—Religious aspects—Christianity. 3. Catholics—Religious life. I. Klausing, Patrice. II. Title.

BV4596.I57Y68 2007
241'.68—dc22
2007015461

ISBN 978-0-86716-804-4

Published by St. Anthony Messenger Press
28 W. Liberty St.
Cincinnati, OH 45202
www.AmericanCatholic.org

Printed in the United States of America.

Printed on acid-free paper.

07 08 09 10 11 5 4 3 2 1

Contents

Introduction

If you are looking at or reading this book, chances are that some, if not all, of the following statements are true: You are concerned about your own or someone else's use of the Internet. You are worried about the effects of this use on a relationship, family life or job performance and security. You fear that there may be no solution to this problem short of a major upheaval in people's lives. You want reliable information based on the best practices that psychology, counseling and addiction studies can provide. You have and want to tap into your own personal spiritual resources to resolve this problem. If these statements resonate within you, then you are one of the people we are hoping to reach out to with this book.

To help facilitate an option for life, we have designed this book to include basic facts and information, how-to measures, anecdotes about the experiences of real people and reflective exercises and prayers to draw upon one's spiritual resources. We have chosen this approach because we are convinced that the most effective recovery process from any addiction is one that is both therapeutically sound and rooted in faith.

It is our hope that this book will offer a foundation, based on fact and faith, which will empower you or your loved one to seek the necessary help. We call it a foundation because research has consistently shown that breaking free of addictive patterns or coping with the addiction of a loved one requires additional support, one that involves a network of people including professional counselors or structured groups, such as Al-Anon or Gamblers Anonymous. So why read this book if it cannot answer all the questions or be the ultimate self-help manual for Internet addiction?

The very first step in dealing with an addiction is to break the pattern of denial, doubt or confusion that one is, in reality, enmeshed in an addictive behavior. In the first part of this book, we address this uncertainty by providing information about addictions in general and Internet addiction in particular. Here you will learn the signs, symptoms and defining behaviors that characterize Internet addiction. We hope that you will also begin to name and deal with the emotional turmoil that addiction causes. Through stories of others who have experienced Internet addiction, we intend to help you normalize your thoughts, feelings and reactions to this addiction.

In the second part of this book, we take a look at the kinds of issues that arise for various groups of people when Internet addiction or abuse is a concern. We examine the effects of online addiction on couples, parents and children, teens and young adults and at the workplace. Recognizing that not everyone is a techno-whiz, we offer some practical guidelines for helping the computer-challenged spouse, parent or friend to achieve at least a basic understanding of and skill with online navigation.

We also use case studies of real people and real situations

from our clinical experience. However, to protect confidentiality, we have either changed information that would identify a client or created a composite character to whom we attribute the experiences of several people.

For people of faith life is brought to prayer and prayer informs life. Allow yourself to interact with the book, to pay attention to the questions it raises, to the answers it provides and to the feelings it generates. Attending to these inspirations of the Holy Spirit can improve your understanding and self-knowledge as can sharing your reflections with a trusted friend or caring mental health professional.

Throughout this book you will find a variety of exercises to help you reflect, pray and tune in to the Spirit of God who prays within us with groaning even when we do not know how to pray (cf. Romans 8:26). When these appear in the text, they will be identified as "Prayer Connections." A Prayer Connection might include a review of church teaching, questions for pondering, Scripture passages related to the topic or a composed prayer. These are offered with the hope that they lead you into your own prayer, that they become avenues by which you may discern the voice of the Spirit who brings forth creation from chaos.

We strongly recommend that you take quiet time to look at this material and to interact with it in different ways: praying the formulated prayers or composing your own; responding to questions in writing; drawing, painting or creatively expressing your thoughts or feelings; meditating on suggested Scriptures; journaling your thoughts and feelings about the text and your own lived experience. For this purpose, we suggest that you use a special notebook, binder or scrapbook in which you can keep your prayer responses private, yet available for your own use. We would also encourage you to attempt the reflections that pique your interest or stretch your horizons, even if you do not believe you have the talent to do the exercise well. It is not the finished product that matters but engaging in the process, opening yourself to truth. Because the world of addiction is filled with lies and deceit, it is of paramount importance that you come to recognize the truth of your own life or of a loved one's struggle because ultimately "the truth will make you free" (John 8:32).

There are always surprises when one undertakes the writing of a book. For us the surprise came as we began to look for church documents that address addiction. The silence is deafening. The problems caused by addiction are mentioned or alluded to in several documents, but there is no substantive work on the topic that we could find. One reason for this may be the incredibly complex factors surrounding addiction. Because one is dealing with addiction (some level of compulsion and lack of freedom), universal moral teaching may not be possible or appropriate. However, addiction issues are rampant in our world, cause much pain and suffering and adversely affect individuals, families and societies. We believe it is time for the church, possibly through the United States Conference of Catholic Bishops (USCCB), to take a comprehensive look at the subject, or at the very least, read this book.

CHAPTER 1

The Silent Addiction

What role does the Internet play in your life? In most cases, the Internet is a productive tool. You can find information, do research, shop and instantly keep in touch with family and friends through electronic mail or make new friends and connections inside online chat rooms. But there is an unintended consequence of this technology, something that observation and recent studies have identified as Internet addiction, a disorder that has silently crept into our homes, schools and businesses.

As the Internet moved quickly to become a daily part of our lives, people started to experience another type of addiction with dramatic consequences. Cheryl, a forty-four-year-old real estate agent explained, "When I got my first computer, I thought the CD player was a cup holder, but within six months, I was spending nearly eighteen hours a day on the thing. My children constantly complained that I tied up the phone line with my modem. I neglected my friends and my family, and I rarely showed homes because that only took time away from the computer. This thing was eating away at my entire life!" Like Cheryl, old and new users alike have experienced the gravitational pull of cyberspace.

Internet addiction isn't something that we think of as a real addiction. In fact, when the coauthor of this book, Kimberly Young, started to study Internet addiction in 1994, most people laughed when she told them what she did. Even now some people still snicker, but it is an all-too-real condition.

When we hear the word *addiction*, we often think of physical addictions to drugs or alcohol, something involving the use of an intoxicant that creates a chemical dependency. However, in the past few decades, researchers have identified another kind of addiction. They call this phenomenon *process addiction*. Process addictions involve dysfunctional patterns and observable addictive symptoms that cluster around certain behaviors, such as eating, gambling, sex, relationships, shopping and spending. Process addictions impact people's lives in the same way physical addictions do, affecting our marriages, our jobs and our personal well-being because we are consumed with a particular behavior—consumed to the point it becomes addictive. The addictive process:

- is a recognizable psychological and behavioral syndrome;
- expresses itself in a particular individual in relationship to specific substances or processes;
- exhibits a striking similarity and commonality among addicted individuals regardless of their specific circumstances and particular addictions.

To help understand the psychological hook of online compulsivity, we first explore the underlying dynamic of process addictions.

PROCESS ADDICTIONS

Stanton Peele, a noted authority on addictive behavior, explained "addictions provide a psychological hook that gives you feelings and gratifying sensations that you are not able to get in other ways."[1] According to Peele addictions accomplish something for the person, however illusory or momentary these benefits may actually be. Because of the mental pleasure that people find in their addictions, they begin to behave more intensely about them. Addiction, therefore, isn't limited to the ingestion of a drug or product that used over a prolonged period of time will result in a chemical dependency or physical need. Addiction also refers to maladaptive behaviors that provide compulsive escape from the problems in people's lives.[2]

Whether one's addiction is to a substance (alcohol, licit or illicit drugs or chemical product) or a process, crossover, switching of addictions, multiple addictions and a changing pattern of addiction are common but not universal features of an underlying addictive illness. Whether the addiction is single or multiple, substance or process, legal or illegal or an unstable and shifting combination of all the above, certain recurring and recognizable common features distinguish addictive from nonaddictive processes.

Characteristics of the addictive process are:

Salience: Occurs when the activity or drug becomes the most important activity in a person's life.

Mood modification: Occurs when one's physical state alters, as in feeling buzzed, high, numb or tranquil when on a drug or engaged in an addictive activity.

Tolerance: When one requires an increased amount of the substance or activity over time to produce the same euphoric effect, one's tolerance is said to have increased.

Withdrawal symptoms: When one stops taking a substance or participating in an addictive activity, unpleasant feelings—physical and mental—most likely occur.

Conflict: As a result of the addictive chemical or activity, often interpersonal and intrapersonal conflicts occur.

Relapse: Occurs when the tendency to repeatedly revert to earlier pathological patterns of use re-emerges, and for the most extreme patterns of use to be quickly restored after many years of control or abstinence.[3]

Reviewing these characteristics, we see that core patterns of behaviors are associated with the addiction process. Whether a substance or process addiction, addicts become consumed with the activity or drug, using it as a form of escape and relief from existing problems in their lives. We see that addicts will rely upon the activity or drug to alter mood, a key motivator driving the addiction and that unpleasant feelings occur when forced to go without it, leading to withdrawal and frequent relapse.

Roger, a thirty-three-year-old computer engineer, explained, "Being online felt like a drug high. I was hooked on online games, and every time I played *EverQuest*, I felt completely absorbed in this online fantasy world. My wife yelled at me every night because I hardly spent any time with her, my kids hated that I tied up the computer, and it started to affect my work. I skipped meetings, missed deadlines, and once I called in sick just to stay home and play *EverQuest*. It got so bad that my wife of eighteen years threatened to leave me and my boss fired me when he found out I was playing the game at work. For me the Internet became more than just a fascination; it was an addiction."

Addictive fascination has been justly compared to the more commonly known stage of romantic or infatuated love in which the lover thinks constantly of the beloved and pines and suffers when not in his or her presence. An individual in such a state of mind is said to be obsessed with his love object and subordinates every other aspect of his existence, including at times his health, work and other relationships to the fulfillment of the almost unbearable need and longing to be united with his beloved. And we know from life, as well as literature, that so passionate and frequently desperate are such lovers that at times they even die or kill as a consequence of or for their love.

Anyone who understands the terrific drive and intensity that underlies and propels well-established addictive illness will not be surprised at the difficulties individuals encounter when attempting to control or terminate their addictive behaviors. In such situations the biblical quote, "the spirit indeed is willing, but the flesh is weak" is an apt description of affairs once the individual has reached the stage of recognizing his addiction and the need to do something about it (Matthew 26:41). In many, if not most cases, addicts recognize the harmful nature of their behavior only very late in the course of the addictive process, attempting to conceal it and making the problems created by the addiction worse.

PRAYER CONNECTIONS

• As you finish reading this section on the signs of addiction, what fears have surfaced? Write down the fears of which you are aware. How do you feel as you look at your fears?

• Ponder the following Scriptures:

> [D]o not fear, for I am with you,
>> do not be afraid, for I am your God;
> I will strengthen you, I will help you.... (Isaiah 41:10)

> Do not fear, for I have redeemed you;
>> I have called you by name, you are mine.
> When you pass through the waters, I will be with you;
>> and through the rivers, they shall not overwhelm you;
> when you walk through fire you shall not be burned,
>> and the flame shall not consume you.
> For I am the LORD your God, the Holy One of Israel, your
>> Savior. (Isaiah 43:1–3)

> There is no fear in love, but perfect love casts out fear....
> (1 John 4:18)

• Whose perfect love casts out all fear? Journal your responses, feelings or questions to the above readings. Listen to or sing "Be Not Afraid," which was recorded by the St. Louis Jesuits.

THE GRAVITATIONAL PULL

Similar to an alcoholic who needs to consume greater levels of alcohol in order to achieve satisfaction, online addicts need to spend progressively longer amounts of time online. Furthermore, addicts will go to great lengths to mask the nature of their online activities, primarily to conceal the extent and nature of the behavior. In most cases of process addiction, an individual's compulsion is often associated with increasingly painful states of tension and agitation that is only relieved through the completion of the act. For example, an alcoholic is driven to drink or an overeater is driven to binge on food during moments of tension and anxiety. Similarly, as with other addictive disorders, uncomfortable emotional states, negative thoughts or stressful situations can all serve to trigger online binges.

EMOTIONAL STATES

Feelings such as depression, hopelessness or pessimism can drive the alcoholic to drink or the overeater to eat. The addictive behavior itself acts as a way to temporarily avoid these feelings. Under the influence the alcoholic feels as if all the other problems in her life disappear, and when eating, the overeater experiences a sense of peace and relaxation, lessening the overwhelming stress and frustration she feels.

Addictions create a numbing effect. The alcoholic becomes numb to his feelings and perceptions, thus creating a false sense of security. The apparent benefits produced by this positive, altered state reinforces his drinking, long before a physical dependency has set in. The overeater is most vulnerable to bingeing during moments of tension, and eating becomes a way to find comfort and relief from the pressures in life. In each case the compulsive behavior serves to reduce the underlying emotional tension, and similarly, an Internet addict's use of the computer is less about using it as an information tool and more about finding a psychological escape to cope with difficult and painful feelings.

Like a craving for a cigarette or the desire to have a drink, emotions such as stress, depression, loneliness, anxiety or burnout can lead to an addict's need to go online, which serves as a temporary distraction to fill an emotional void. Online addicts explain that they feel a difference between online and offline emotions. They feel frustrated, worried, angry, anxious and depressed when offline. When online, they feel excited, thrilled, uninhibited, attractive, supported and more desirable. These strong positive emotions reinforce the compulsive behavior.

NEGATIVE THOUGHTS

Addictive thinkers often feel apprehensive because they frequently anticipate disaster, even when there is no logical reason for doing so. While addicts are not the only people who worry and anticipate negative happenings, they tend to do this more often than other people. Internet addicts engage in this same type of catastrophic thinking and suffer from a constant stream of negative thoughts that lead to low self-esteem. These harmful thought patterns include all or nothing thinking, magnification of personal problems and selectively interpreting negative events and referring those to themselves. In particular, Internet addicts tend to dwell on negative events and immediate outcomes, fail to make accurate internal attributions, have low rates of self-reinforcement and high rates of self-punishment. However, online they create a virtual life that provides a subjective escape to avoid real or perceived problems. Virtually, the addict feels more confident, possesses a greater self-regard and achieves a more optimistic self-evaluation. This relieves feelings of personal inadequacy and deep core beliefs about themselves, such as "I am no good," or "I am a failure." However, relief is only temporary, so the act is repeated.

STRESSFUL SITUATIONS

According to Peele a person is vulnerable to addiction when she feels a lack of satisfaction in her life, an absence of intimacy or strong connection to others, a lack of self-confidence or compelling interests or a loss of hope.[4] In a similar manner, individuals who are dissatisfied with or upset by a particular area or multiple areas of their lives have an increased likelihood of developing Internet addiction because they don't have any other way of coping. For example, instead of making positive choices to directly address a marital problem, job dissatisfaction, medical illness, unemployment or academic instability, Internet addicts will typically go online for hours. This serves to dull the pain, avoid the problem and maintain the status quo. When they log offline, they realize that their difficulties have not changed. Nothing is altered by Internet use, yet it appears easier to jump online than to deal with the difficult or overwhelming life issues head-on. Such substitution for missing needs often allows the addicts to temporarily escape their problems, but the substitute behaviors are not the means to solve the root of the real underlying problems in their lives.

A DOWNWARD SPIRAL

The longer the person is away from the Internet, the more intense such unpleasant feelings become. Therefore, the driving force for many online addicts is the relief gained by engaging in the Internet. And because addictions serve a useful purpose for the addict, the attachment or sensation may grow to such proportions that it damages a person's life.

These feelings translate into cues that cultivate a psychological longing for the euphoria associated with the Internet that enables a person to forget or feel OK about some insurmountable problem. The Internet provides an artificial, temporary feeling of security or calm, of self-worth or accomplishment, of power and control or intimacy or belonging. Therefore, the Internet blocks out sensations of pain, uncertainty or discomfort by creating powerfully distracting sensations that focus and absorb attention. It is these perceived benefits that explain why a person keeps coming back to the addictive experience. When they are forced to go without it, addicts experience withdrawal, panic and even racing, obsessive thoughts, such as, "I must have it"; "I can't go without it"; "I need it."

Elizabeth worked as a history teacher for a community college outside of Detroit. At thirty-eight she spent her nights in front of the computer reading sites on historical figures to help prepare her classes and scanning Web sites on gardening, her one true passion. One night she discovered a chat room for gardeners. "It started innocently enough," Elizabeth explains. "Out of curiosity, I talked with a few of the members. We had so much in common, and soon they became my closest friends. I didn't eat, didn't sleep. All I did was chat and instant message (IM). Whenever I felt stressed at work, had a fight with my boyfriend, or when I found out my mother was diagnosed with cancer, it was the one safe place in my life where I could turn. It's like I disappeared into this virtual world that didn't demand much from me, but gave me all kinds of acceptance. But really all it did was make my life worse. My boyfriend left me, my friends stopped calling, and I was hanging on to my job by a shoestring. I even tried to get my boyfriend to go online just so he'd stay, but he wanted nothing to do with it. He wanted me to give it up, but I needed it too much. When it comes right down to it, I wouldn't give it up, not even for him."

Ask yourself the following questions and see what patterns emerge:

- What time of day do you usually go online?
- Do you log online the first thing in the morning?
- Do you deprive yourself of sleep to stay online?
- How long do you typically stay online?
- Are you online for just a few minutes or for a few hours?
- How do you feel just before you log online?
- Are you stressed, annoyed or tense, but feel more relaxed, less irritable or less anxious when online?
- Do you ever use the Internet to forget other problems going on in your life, perhaps a recent fight with a spouse, a disagreement with a coworker or a bad day at school?
- Does being online make you momentarily forget about these problems? Or does it in some way help you cope with them?
- How do you feel when you are offline?
- Do you ever miss or crave the Internet?

PRAYER CONNECTIONS

God of Wisdom, you have charged us with being stewards of the earth. In our desire to explore, create and invent, we have produced marvels that are reflections of your purpose for humanity. But we often cannot control what we have made. So today I praise you for the blessings that the Internet has brought to so many, and I ask for your grace in conquering its dark side in my life. In the Internet you have placed before me the blessing and the curse: Let me choose life that I may observe your Law and truly live. (Cf. Deuteronomy 30:13–20)

The Warning Signs

As experts in this field we are often asked, "How much time online is too much?" It isn't simply a matter of time. We can't say ten hours a week online is OK, but eleven hours is too much no more than we can diagnose alcoholism by counting the number of drinks someone consumes. We can't say that ten drinks a week is okay, but eleven or more is a sign of addiction.

Trying to diagnose any addiction is complex. When does anything become too much? When does drinking become an addiction? When does eating become a disorder? When do certain sexual behaviors become problematic? Clinicians say one clear sign of an addiction is that the behavior escalates until it is out of control. The user can't stop or doesn't know how, despite the problems the behavior is causing in her life. Internet addiction has these same qualities. There is a loss of control, and life has become unmanageable, yet the addict cannot give up the Internet. It has become the primary relationship in the addict's life.

The warning signs of Internet addiction may be subtle. It may be that you feel you are still in control over your Internet use, but find that you are starting to feel dependent upon being online. You think about it even when you are offline and eagerly anticipate when you can be online next. It may be that you recently met someone online and can't wait to check your e-mail to see if this new friend has written. And now you find that you are checking your e-mail ten, twelve, fifteen times a day. One mother of three explained, "I didn't realize I even had a habit until one day I forgot to pick my kids up at school because I was too busy chatting with my online friends. It was then that I realized how much the Internet had taken hold of my life. Every night, once I tuck the kids into bed, I'm online, staying up all hours, too exhausted to get them ready for school, cook them dinner, spend any real quality time with them, and now I'm too busy to even remember to pick them up. While I can't say that I felt addicted, I realized that I was turning into a complete failure as a mother because of it."

While time is not a direct function in diagnosing Internet addiction, addicts generally are excessive about their online usage, spending anywhere from forty to eighty hours per week online. Sleep patterns are disrupted due to late-night log-ins, and addicts generally stay up surfing until two, three or four in the morning even when faced with the reality of having to wake up early for work or school. In extreme cases caffeine pills are used to facilitate longer Internet sessions. Such sleep depravation causes excessive fatigue that in turn impairs academic or occupational performance and may harm the immune system, leaving the addict vulnerable to disease. Furthermore, sitting at the computer for such prolonged periods also means that addicts aren't getting proper exercise and are at increased risk for back strain, carpal tunnel syndrome and other medical conditions.

When everyone is using the Internet as a part of their daily lives, isn't it hard to tell the difference between healthy and unhealthy patterns of use? In our technologically driven culture, the Internet has permeated every aspect of our lives: We shop, do research, make reservations, pay bills and send e-mail. Using the Internet to carry out these tasks of daily living is the way we do business, but it can also mask the warning signs of online addiction. So then how can you tell if you or a loved one may suffer from an addiction? To help as a guide, consider how you have come to use the Internet and ask yourself the following questions:

- Do you frequently stay online longer than you originally intended?
- Do you find it difficult to control your Internet use?
- Have you lied to family members, therapists or others to conceal the extent of your involvement with the Internet?
- Do you feel preoccupied with using the Internet?
- Do you use the Internet as a way of escaping other problems or issues in your life?
- Do you feel depressed, anxious or irritable if you are forced to go without the Internet even for short periods of time?
- Do you continue to use the Internet despite problems it is causing in your life?
- Have significant people in your life voiced their concern about your Internet use or complained about the amount of time you spend online?

Becoming addicted to the Internet can be just as devastating as becoming addicted to alcohol or drugs. While a physical dependency isn't present, the same interpersonal and social problems are. Isolation, depression, divorce, job loss, academic problems, financial problems and physical problems can all be caused by online addiction.

Early in Kimberly's career she met Alex. At sixteen he struggled to fit in at school. He was a loner by his parents' standards, and when they divorced, he went into a deep depression. Alex's father bought him a new computer. He quickly took to it and to the Internet. Because he lived with his mother out in the country, it was a long-distance phone call to dial into America Online (AOL). When his mother received a phone bill for eight hundred dollars, she asked Alex to stop using the Internet. He agreed, but when she received another phone bill for the same amount of money the next month, she removed the modem from his computer. Alex bought a new one and the next month, another eight-hundred-dollar phone bill arrived. His mother took the phone jack out of his room, so Alex bought wiring from K-Mart and ran it to the telephone pole in front of the house. His mother dismantled the computer and locked it in her closet.

Alex had a complete breakdown. He wouldn't eat, didn't sleep, constantly trembled and started to chew on paper cups. His mother, terrified for her son's well-being, started to call around looking for child psychologists, therapists, counselors—anyone who knew about Internet addiction. Before she found the help she needed, Alex found a pistol that his mother kept in the house for protection. When she came home from work one night, according to the police report, Alex shot his mother five times, killing her. He went into the bathroom, vomited and then shot and killed himself. It was a chilling story when Kimberly first heard it, and a chilling story even as she writes about it today. Although it is an extreme case, it illustrates the depth and power an Internet addiction can have, how psychological dependency on the Internet can quickly form, how people can rely upon this technology as more than just a productive tool and how it can become a way of life—a way of life that can have devastating effects if one is forced to do without it.

INFORMATION OVERLOAD

Not everyone who goes online may experience these symptoms or warning signs to an extreme. Often you may go online without any real problem or need to stay online. Perhaps you feel overwhelmed by the constant surge of electronic noise in your life, and instead of feeling like technology has helped you do more, you do more because of it.

Because the Internet provides such easy access to the outside world, we are constantly tempted to connect to the office, to coworkers and to colleagues without ever giving ourselves a chance to fully relax. Because the Internet never sleeps, we can go online at any hour of the day or night, hooking us to something that can potentially take away from quality time that we might otherwise spend with our spouse, our children or our neighbors. Our patterns of Internet use might leave us little time to work on crafts, go golfing or do the things we used to enjoy because our time is now spent "connected" online. Technology has a purpose, and a good purpose, but when taken to the extreme it can destroy the relationships in our lives. We spend more time with our virtual lives, checking e-mail, reading Web sites and chatting with online friends, and less and less time with our real-life family and friends.

Slowly the Internet and the time you spend on it can eat away at important and purposeful relationships, and ultimately one can get so caught up in the web of the Internet that it is difficult to break free. The wealth of data available on the World Wide Web has created something called *technostress*, whereby you may feel overwhelmed by all the new technology. You spend long hours in front of the computer getting lost in searching and collecting data from the Web and organizing and reorganizing information instead of spending time with your husband or wife or going out with friends. Because technology lets you do more, you can take on too much and end up feeling overwhelmed and never really "finished" because you are constantly plugged in. While technology helps us be more productive, it can also lead to stress and burnout by letting you work twenty-four hours a day, seven days a week.

As Bob, a forty-eight-year-old attorney, explains, "Even when I was away on family vacations, I had to check my voice mail and e-mail, and my cell phone was never far away. My wife hated my job and thought it was what was making me do this, but it was all me. I had to have the latest gadget and couldn't even think about living without my BlackBerry. It didn't matter where I was; I had to be plugged in. We'd be at dinner and my cell would go off three times before we were through appetizers. If I couldn't sleep, I'd get up to check my e-mail, and before my first cup of coffee I'd have to check my BlackBerry. I missed my son's soccer games and my daughter's swim meets, and it wasn't until my wife wanted to leave that I realized how much of a workaholic I had become."

CHAPTER SUMMARY QUESTIONS

1. When a spider builds a web, it works from the inside and anchors to the outside, laying down threads that create the basic form. Once it has reached the outer edges, it reverses its direction and consumes this first layer of threads to conserve protein in order to build another web at a later time. As the spider eats these strands, they are replaced with the sticky trap threads that make the web dangerous to other insects. Reflect on and creatively express what feeds your Internet addiction and what problems it creates for you.

2. Take what you have written or created and find a time and space to be alone. Simply hold what you have done, inviting God to enter the mess and the pain.

3. Write or draw ways in which the Internet is a blessing. List ways in which the Internet itself or misuse of the Internet are harmful to society in general and to you personally.

4. What have you learned? What needs to change? What is the next, single, doable step?

CHAPTER 2

What Makes the Internet So Addictive?

No testing has overtaken you that is not common to everyone.
God is faithful, and he will not let you be tested beyond your
strength, but with the testing he will also provide the way out
so that you may be able to endure it.

—1 Corinthians 10:13

The Internet can test our faith. While the Internet is a positive tool for researching information and communicating with others, it also has a dark side. It has a dark side full of arousal, seduction and temptation for unsuspecting users. "Blessed is anyone who endures temptation. Such a one has stood the test and will receive the crown of life that the Lord has promised to those who love him" (James 1:12).

The dark side of the Internet is a world of online pornography, gambling and sexual solicitation. In short, it is an entire virtual underworld that has become an accepted part of the cyberspace culture. Online there are no limitations to what someone can say, post or view. The uncensored nature of cyberspace provides an initial doorway to accessing anything from online pornography, to virtual casinos, to betting sites, to violent games, to sexually explicit chat rooms. In this chapter we explore how the Internet creates new ways of becoming hooked on traditional addictions such as gambling or sex and how it creates new forms of abuse unique to the cyberspace culture.

The Hook of the Internet

What makes the Internet so addictive? Unlike drugs or alcohol, an addiction to the Internet isn't a result of a chemical dependency or an intoxicant that leads to a physical dependency. Long before drug addicts and alcoholics develop a chemical dependency, they experience psychological dependency. They use drugs or alcohol as a means to escape problems or feelings that they aren't able to deal with, and drinking or drug use become ways of avoiding stressful situations or unpleasant feelings. Because the escape is only temporary, more alcohol and more drugs are used to keep avoiding and to keep feeling numb. Emotionally, the drug addict or alcoholic learns to self-medicate, temporarily forgetting and momentarily coping with the pain and stress of life.

As we discussed in the first chapter, Internet addicts use the online world as a psychological escape. The Internet is a seemingly safe way to cope with life's problems, and it is a legal and relatively inexpensive way to soothe or avoid disturbing feelings. Because of this, the Internet can quickly become a convenient means for instantly forgetting whatever stresses and pains an addict is experiencing.

Online Temptation

Not everyone becomes addicted to the Internet for the same reason, nor do they become addicted to the same thing. Unlike addicts to drugs or alcohol, Internet addicts can personalize their addictions by choosing a specific format and by developing a unique coping strategy for dealing with problems. For example, some people find themselves addicted to online pornography, others to online gaming and still others to online shopping. To better illustrate the ways that people can experience Internet addiction, we have identified six problem areas that often lead to an unhealthy or addictive use of the Internet.

1. ONLINE PORNOGRAPHY

With an abundance of sexually explicit material readily available online, a new form of sexual addiction has developed. Characterized by convenience, the appeal of anonymity and an extraordinarily real and graphic nature, this form of addiction feeds on virtual experiences that far surpass what video stores, adult shops or magazines can offer.

Harold, a fifty-two-year-old lawyer who had been married thirty-five years, explains, "I wasn't the kind of man to look much at pornography. Maybe when I was younger, but it wasn't something I had to seek out. One night while working late, I stumbled onto an adult Web site. Soon I was completely hooked. Every time I felt stressed with another deadline at work or assigned a new case, I relaxed by looking at porn sites. I started to miss meetings, miss important deadlines, and I stayed late at the office. Every spare minute I had I was looking at porn. I tried to stop. I kept promising myself I would never do it again. I'd quit for a while, but then the process would start all over again. This pattern continued until one of the partners discovered my habit. I lost my job and my marriage—everything that was important to me."

Online pornography isn't just an addiction problem but a cultural problem as well. Sexually explicit material that was once hard to find is now a mouse click away. We are inundated with spam (junk e-mail) that blatantly advertises adult Web sites, and it is so ubiquitous that we can easily bump into it, even when we aren't looking for it or don't necessarily want it.

Adults, children, anyone using the technology can accidentally find online porn and start browsing through millions of images. Students can sit in computer labs or dorm rooms and find it. Even though they use filters, campuses and schools report that online pornography still gets through the system because the difference between ".gov" and ".com" at the end of a Web address can mean the difference between an informative government site and a pornographic one.

As Harold discovered, his initial urge to look at pornography started with an unintentional visit to a porn site during an otherwise appropriate computer session. As well as being a successful attorney, Harold was also a respected member of the community. "I volunteered at Rotary and was actively involved with my church. I can't tell you how devastated I was when people discovered why my wife left me—all this pain because I just couldn't stop looking at porn. I went into a deep depression that I'm still trying to recover from. I can't figure out why I did it or how it got to be so bad."

PRAYER CONNECTIONS

Harold's sad, though common, story demonstrates the rationale and logic that underpins the church's teaching that Catholics have an obligation to avoid the "near occasions of sin." Occasions of sin are defined as people, places, things or events that move us away from right relationship with God, self, others and all of creation. Stumbling onto a pornographic Web site is not a problem. Returning to that Web site or deliberately seeking out similar sites jeopardizes your capacity to avoid such sites in the future and to choose behaviors consistent with the gospel. What are the people, places, things or events that move you away from a right relationship with God, self, others and creation? What concrete step can you take to begin avoiding these things?

FOR THE ADDICT

Like a spider that catches unsuspecting victims in her web, so the Internet can lure the unwary into harmful situations. Recall the first time you came across a Web site clearly sexual in nature. Remember what your life was like at that time. How was it different? In what way would you want your life to be different now? Take time to write down your thoughts.

FOR THOSE WHO LOVE SOMEONE ADDICTED TO INTERNET PORNOGRAPHY

Loving someone addicted to Internet pornography requires the wisdom of Solomon and the balance of a high-wire tightrope walker. There are two primary temptations: being self-righteous and being condemnatory. The Christian in this situation is well-advised to meditate on the Gospel values of compassion (cf. John 8:2–11) and being nonjudgmental (cf. Luke 6:7–42).

The balancing act becomes more complicated when one faces the issue of becoming or being an enabler of the addict's behavior. Enabling behavior encourages another to repeat certain behaviors because the enabler absorbs or lessens the consequences for the addicted loved one. In our imperfect world, sometimes the only way to get an addict's attention is to physically and emotionally withdraw support. Severing a relationship is a major decision with long-term consequences and should not be undertaken without due prayer and discernment. As with the early church, the person who finds himself or herself with no other recourse except breaking the bonds of relationship must do so with the hope that the isolation will eventually bring about healing.

2. Adult Chat Rooms

Beyond online pornography there are explicitly sexual adult chat rooms. With this type of access, cyberspace allows people to dabble, experiment and explore sexual feelings and indulge in private fantasies unique to the online environment. As one woman explains, "I started talking in sex chat rooms out of curiosity, and eventually I began to enjoy this experience more than having sex with my husband."

In cyberspace these on-demand, fantasy-themed, role-play chat rooms cater to any sexual desire or need imaginable. If a man desires to have sex with a virgin, he can enter the "Virgin in Waiting" chat room. If a woman wonders what it would be like to be with an older man, she can enter the "Older Men for Younger Women" chat room. Sadly, even deviant sexual practices, such as fetishes, bondage, bestiality, sadism and masochism, incest, rape and even child sexual abuse can be vividly experienced. In short, if you can think of a particular sexual scenario, there is probably a Web site to accommodate it.

For the addict, the fantasy theme begins and progresses much like a novel. A cast of characters is created with the people in the specific type of chat room entered. Through typed dialogue, online users privately message each other, sharing their innermost sexual fantasies. Participants personalize their sexual fantasies to the degree that they become a character in their own self-created erotic novel. This experience of sharing sexual fantasies or needs or of receiving sexual gratification online is commonly known as *cybersex*.

Such computer-enabled fantasies are highly reinforcing; they perpetuate and strengthen the need to repeat the behavior. The addict's preoccupation with sexual arousal stems from his own imagination and fantasy history. The association of the Internet with sexual arousal is so potent that it transforms the Internet from a practical business or research device into a modern-day sex toy. Sometimes just recalling the potent images of one's last cybersex episode triggers arousal and reinforces the notion that cyberspace is an open gateway for immediate sexual gratification and fulfillment.

Barbara's story illustrates the point. She is a fifty-one-year-old teacher and grandmother who got involved with sado-masochistic chat rooms. Raised Mormon in rural Utah, she had never been able to express or act upon her desire to be controlled by men. She led a conservative lifestyle and conformed to her church teachings, except when she went online. "My whole world changed when I discovered the Internet," she explains. "Since high school I always wanted to be completely dominated by a man, but I hid my desires because I feared that I would lose the respect of the men I dated. They were always good Mormon boys—including my husband who would simply die if he knew I liked this type of thing. For the first time in my life, I can act upon fantasies I kept bottled up inside of me." As Barbara learned, this form of online sex can have devastating effects. Freely and indiscriminately exploring hidden or repressed sexual fantasies can unlock a whirlwind of behaviors that cannot easily be contained. In Barbara's case fantasy was a major component of her online sexuality. Through the Internet she explored repressed and latent sexual feelings that she had kept buried for so long. Once she unleashed them, she didn't know how to deal with or confront these feelings, yet she could not tear herself away from the activity that fed her confusion and pain.

As users become more comfortable with technology and with cybersex, they start to experience predictable changes in their behavior. These changes serve as warning signs that a person has become hooked:

- He routinely spends significant amounts of time in chat rooms and sends private messages with the sole purpose of finding cybersex.
- She feels preoccupied with using the Internet to find online sexual partners.
- He frequently uses anonymous communication to engage in sexual fantasies not typically carried out in real life.
- She anticipates the next online session with the expectation that she will find sexual arousal or gratification.
- He frequently moves from cybersex to phone sex (or even real-life meetings).

- She hides her online interactions from her significant others.
- He feels guilt or shame about his online use.
- She is less invested with her real-life sexual partner because she has come to prefer cybersex as her primary form of sexual gratification.

If you recognize that these behaviors describe *you*, now is the time to reach out for professional help. Overcoming online sexual addiction is not a battle that can be easily won, and it is rarely won in isolation. If you love someone who exhibits these behaviors, seek help for yourself so that you can maintain your own sense of balance and well-being and can avoid falling into the trap of enabling another's addiction.

PRAYER CONNECTIONS

In discussing online sex, we in no way mean to imply that coming in touch with one's own sexuality is wrong, bad or sinful. There are a fair number of people who need to integrate their sexuality into their emotional and spiritual lives, but this healthy exploration of sexuality is a conscious choice for wholeness and healing and is most often undertaken with a caring, knowledgeable companion (counselor, spiritual director or other trusted, competent friend) in a safe and nurturing environment. One resource for doing this is *Created in God's Image* by Carl Koch.

3. CHAT ROOMS IN GENERAL

The very nature of chat rooms allows users to develop screen names or "handles" that mask the true identity of all who meet in the anonymous world of cyberspace. Anonymity is very powerful and one of the most seductive lures of the Internet. Users feel less intimidated and more confident interacting with electronic friends within virtual contexts. This can be an especially important and attractive feature for overly shy or self-conscious individuals. Users can explore or adopt new online personas that radically and qualitatively differ from their real-life personalities because there is no accountability, no face-to-face encounter, no I-Thou relationship. For example, a quiet and reserved person may voice opinions or confront, challenge and dominate others within virtual environments because she feels protected behind the anonymity of the computer screen. Anonymity allows and encourages some users to sexually experiment because all conventional wisdom, messages, values and mores about sex are eliminated online. Anonymity thus provides users with a unique environment for exploring hidden or repressed fantasies and makes it possible to compartmentalize one's sexuality.

Behind the Computer Screen
Psychological research has repeatedly shown that people tend to do things in private or in crowds that they would never do alone in public. At a rock concert, people act differently and feel less inhibited than they would at home, on the job or while shopping. In a new city or on vacation, a person can pretend to be someone else by making up a new name, lifestyle, job and age. This false persona can be shared with people a person meets at the airport, on a bus, in a casino or at the other end of a bar. Living out the "new you" creates an escape from reality, even if for a moment. Depending on a person's intent in using a false identity, such behavior may indeed be harmless as long as he stays connected to his own reality.

Now consider what happens when the same scenario is applied to the Internet. From behind the computer screen, a person can create a virtual reality that is not at all consistent with how she relates to and acts toward others in real life. She can change her name, age, occupation, education, gender, physical appearance—anything is possible over the Internet because the checks and balances that we rely on in a physical encounter do not exist. In person, if someone tells you he is twenty-five and the physical evidence is screaming "more like fifty-five!" you have some way to evaluate and judge the information given. When a person goes online, he can share whatever information he wants with millions of invisible strangers who have no way to and sometimes no interest in verifying the truth of his statements.

Julie, a thirty-eight-year-old homemaker and mother of three explains, "I met dozens of new friends in online chat rooms for gardening, which is my passion." Each day she chatted for hours and ventured into new rooms with more potential online friends. "I felt like a different person online," she explains. "I was much more open and more popular. People started asking me all kinds of questions. I became the guru of gardening. Then I started making up things about myself. It started with little things. I told them I was a master gardener, which I wasn't, and told them that I had this enormous garden, which I didn't. As I became more confident, I began to make new friends in new rooms and made up an entirely different life. One day I was an innkeeper in Maine. The next day I was a carefree coed who lived in California and roller-bladed along the beach. Part of the thrill was seeing how far I could go, and how much people would believe, but it started to affect me. Soon I wasn't speaking to my gardening friends anymore. Instead, I spent hours making up elaborate stories. There was this incredible power attached to becoming someone completely different every day and leading a life that seemed more interesting and more fulfilling than my own."

Because of the anonymity factor in online chat rooms, meeting people online is a completely different experience than meeting people in real life. When you meet people online, they can't see you and only know you by what you tell them. You are judged by how you type, the words you choose, and you are in complete control to reveal as much or as little as you want. You can tell others that you are older, younger, thinner or taller. You can tell others that you live in any part of the world, or that you are richer or better looking than you really are. You can tell them that you live alone when you are married. You can tell them that you don't have children when you have just finished tucking your little ones in bed. You can tell them you work as a doctor when you are a plumber, or that you are a tall blonde when you are a short redhead.

New Identities

When do these small white lies turn into something more than just a fantasy? At first it may seem harmless to make up a new name, new age or new occupation. It might be fun to make up a new life, an imaginary life, something that only exists inside the computer. It might make you seem more interesting or more glamorous. It might make you feel excited to pretend to be younger or thinner or wealthier. But when does that fantasy turn into a habit, into something much more dangerous or addictive?

The capacity to imagine and pretend is foundational to our human growth and development as individuals and as a society.

Pretending and imagining can empower us to bring about significant and beneficial changes in our lives, in our world. The ability to make up false identities or to play out a fantasy is not of itself indicative of a problem. The issue becomes problematic when these false identities are so constantly practiced and so highly reinforced that they become more real inside the mind of an online user than the truth of his life.

Making up false identities online gives you the ability to create a different mental image of yourself, some idealized version of the truth, or a completely new identity that can alter how you look at what is real in your life. You can start to look at your real life as dull, boring or routine. You start to feel as if you are in a rut or that real life seems very ordinary. This is a dangerous comparison for a person to make. Gradually, the online life assumes greater importance than real life, and the person starts to feel disenchanted with and disappointed by ordinary human experience. So he withdraws into the secret fantasy life inside the computer. It no longer seems like a fantasy, and he likes who he is on the computer. He prefers spending time online, with new online friends who think he is wittier, more attractive or more interesting than how he believes real people perceive him. He immerses himself in a world of new friends, more people, and most likely spends hours seeking better ways of starting online conversations. The virtual world no longer seems like a pretend place, but a fully developed and desirable life accessible only through the computer.

The computer then holds a deeper meaning, a more significant existence inside of it. It is no longer a machine capable of doing word processing, finding information or storing files, but it is a virtual life with its own set of norms, relationships and activities.

Julie had found herself at an emotional and spiritual cross-roads as she became more immersed in her secret virtual fantasy life. "My husband constantly yelled that I was on the computer. I couldn't tell him or the kids what I was really doing. I found myself on it the moment I put my children on the bus for school. I could go online and be anybody I wanted. Men especially found me to be more interesting and attractive. It became an outlet for the routine of my life. My husband was a workaholic, and I had quit my job in marketing to stay home and take care of the kids. Don't get me wrong. I love my husband and children, but online it was like this separate existence, a place where I could be the woman whom I always fantasized being, someone more glamorous and more exciting. Men found me witty and charming, and I knew this was hurting my marriage, but I didn't care. My husband and I were having problems. I resented giving up my career so he could pursue his. It wasn't until Eric discovered my chatroom logs that my fantasy life collided with reality. He was furious —he had bought software and had been monitoring me for weeks. As I stared at the hard, cold evidence, I couldn't believe how I had completely compromised my own values and got so tangled up by the computer."

PRAYER CONNECTIONS

The very nature of God is rooted in relationship. Catholics believe that our God is Trinity in Unity. The presence of Father, Son and Spirit to one another and their eternal interaction is the source of a love so powerful that it creates, redeems and makes all holy. During his life on earth, Jesus of Nazareth gathered people together and formed them into a community of disciples. Saint Paul teaches that Jesus himself is the source of our being brother and sister to one another because he is our brother.

The false personas and intent to deceive that characterize most Internet relationships go against a basic Divine and human instinct: the desire to disclose, to reveal oneself and to lovingly receive the disclosure and revelation of another. Perhaps part of the restlessness, shame and guilt that an Internet addict feels stems from this being out of sync with what is so intrinsic and sacred. The following prayer expresses a desire to return to right relationship.

> Most Gracious, Triune God,
> teach me the value of being in right relationship
> with you, with myself, with others and with all of creation.
> Give me strength to turn away from all that leads to isolation
> and disharmony.
> Give me courage to embrace the truth of my own identity
> and the grace to be open and honest in all of my relation-
> ships.
> Amen.

4. ONLINE GAMING

While not as prevalent as addictions to cyberporn or online chatting, addiction to interactive online gaming has grown substantially over the last decade. A take-off on the old *Dungeons and Dragons* games, often known as Multi-User Dungeons, (MUDs), interactive gaming draws upon power, dominance and recognition within a role-playing, make-believe virtual world. As in chat rooms, users create screen names or handles but are only known to each other through character roles in the game. Men are more attracted to these role-playing games in which they assume a character role associated with specific skills, attributes and rankings that fellow players acknowledge and treat accordingly.

MUDs differ from traditional video arcade games. Instead of a player's eye-hand coordination improving, the actual strength, skills and rankings of the character improve. MUD players earn respect and recognition from fellow players, and younger men, especially those with low self-esteem and poor relationship skills, are at the greatest risk of becoming addicted, especially if they develop a powerful persona within the game.

Michael, a college sophomore addicted to a MUD game called *Medievia*, explains, "At first I liked my character, Morpheus, and it was like being somebody really important. The game involved a lot of skill and strategy, and I was good at the game. Other players respected me. I spent hours exploring new places and fighting new battles. It didn't feel like this place was inside my computer and it became a part of me. I had a whole life online. I had friends; I had a girlfriend; it was everything that my real life wasn't. Outside the game, I didn't have many friends, and I rarely dated. I had never excelled at school, but in the game, all that changed."

Today interactive gaming has taken on new themes that go beyond *Dungeons and Dragons*. They are easier to learn and appeal to a wider audience. *EverQuest* is perhaps one of the fastest growing multi-user games to gain popularity with the mainstream public, and it appears to equally attract both men and women.

Gaming also encompasses traditional board games such as Yahtzee or bingo. There is an interactive, social component when playing these games online that often does not exist in the real world. The user comes to rely on this fantasy world for personal validation and for meeting social needs. The reality of life can disappear with a click of a button.

"My mother constantly plays games online," one woman explains. "She didn't even know how to use the computer when we first bought it, and now she spends every waking moment playing bingo. She says she isn't always playing but chatting with her new online friends. My father and I can't even get on the computer. What's worse, the computer is in my room. I have to kick her out, sometimes at two or three the morning."

Clearly this woman's addiction to online bingo was jeopardizing her marriage and family relationships. As with other forms of Internet addiction, interactive gaming has led to divorce, job loss and health problems.

5. Online Gambling

Online casinos have sprung up practically overnight into a multimillion-dollar business, attracting a large number of gamblers worldwide. Compulsive gambling has been around for centuries, but now access and opportunity are even greater with the invention of Internet gambling, bringing with it a new form of addictive behavior.

Jason is a thirty-two-year-old attorney who just graduated from law school. He dabbled in online gambling while he worked his way through school, but his addiction didn't fully manifest itself until he started working at a law firm in New York. He describes his life at the time: "I just got married and felt the pressures of starting at the firm. I was working eighty hours a week, studying for the bar exam, coming home exhausted, only to get up early to do it all over again the next day. I started gambling online when I got home as a way to relax, then at work as a break from the stress. Soon the money I spent ballooned into an incredible habit. I took out loans just to gamble and lied to my wife, who must've thought I was having an online affair. I was at the computer every night and spent all of our savings. I tried to stop so many times because I knew I couldn't afford it, but the Internet was always there. I worried my boss would find out, and every time I logged offline, I promised to quit. I hated myself for all the wasted time and money and played mind games, like telling myself just a little wouldn't hurt. I wore myself down, and the whole process started all over again. I felt defeated as the temptation was constant and relapse was just a click away."

The global nature of the Internet, combined with the limited, if not impossible, ability of local governments to effectively regulate or ban online gambling, has significant social consequences. Today all anyone needs is a computer and the Internet to access the thousands of available online casinos. The twenty-four-hours-a-day, seven-days-a-week availability of online casinos simulates the seductive and realistic experience of the traditional casino that lures millions of new users each year. Online gambling creates new concerns because the anonymity and privacy of gambling from one's own home makes it more attractive and is easily accessible to children and teenagers as well as to adults.

Brad, a nineteen-year-old math major at the University of Minnesota lost his scholarship and had to quit school because of his addiction to online gambling. "I didn't start out thinking I would get so hooked," he explained. "I started playing 'Texas Hold 'Em' after watching a poker show on TV. It was just something I did for fun. Then I started staying up late, missing classes, spending tons of money; all my time was spent playing the game. It was more than winning and losing money. To be a good player, you've got to be smart, and I liked the intellectual challenge and competitiveness of the game."

Brad's mother became concerned when she discovered Brad's falling grades. "I knew it was about the computer," she said. "But no one seemed to believe me. A counselor at his school told me that it was just a phase." Parents and spouses are usually the first to notice a loved one's online gambling habit and the range of behaviors is similar to those for any type of gambling addiction. These behaviors include:

- showing increased excitement when going online to find new gambling spots;
- rearranging schedules to permit more time for online gambling activities;
- feeling that a change in online gambling activities will bring good luck and subsequently increasing the size of their bets;
- chasing lost bets to try to catch up;
- placing larger bets and betting more frequently;
- boasting about winning and minimizing losses;
- going online to gamble when faced with a crisis or a stressful situation.

In addition to the above symptoms, there are changes in the person's personality and routine behaviors. Suddenly there are unexplained absences from work, home or other responsibilities. The person becomes secretive, conceals or attempts to conceal her time spent at the computer, and outright lies about the real nature of her computer activity. Often the gambling addict experiences mood swings, showing extreme highs when she wins and extreme lows when she loses. Values go by the wayside and many violate their own principles. They begin to hide money, take secret loans or make sporadic and unexplained withdrawals from family bank accounts. Suddenly they find themselves capable of or actually stealing money from friends and family—then lying about it—in order to bet more, pay off debts or recoup losses.

If you see yourself in this, you very likely suffer from compulsive online gambling. Take a moment to reflect on how online gambling has affected your life. Consider both the personal and financial losses. Have you hidden betting losses and lied to family and friends about what you are doing on the computer? Have you experienced the thrill of winning and return to betting as a way of coping with problems and stressful situations? Are you ashamed of your behavior or fearful of the possible consequences of your unbridled gambling? If so, you may need professional help. We suggest that you contact Gamblers Anonymous as the first step toward reclaiming your life.

A special word of caution needs to be spoken here about the now prolific "non-gambling" sites that have sprung up and that are widely advertised through Internet pop-ups and on radio and television. These sites promise that you will learn how to play poker or blackjack or craps like a pro; in fact, you'll have the opportunity to interact with some of the professional players and learn from them. You also have the opportunity to win prizes—often vacations to real casino locales—and it doesn't cost a penny. Although these sites are not technically gambling sites, they introduce thousands of people to traditional gambling games, and some success in the non-wagered game can often lead one to think that she can translate that success into large winnings in a "real" game. In moral theology this on-the-edge choice is known as "the slippery slope." Unfortunately, it does not take much of a push for one to find oneself buried at the bottom of a gambling addiction that began with a "harmless" non-betting site.

6. EBAY ADDICTION AND OTHER ONLINE COMPULSIONS

Manifesting behavior patterns similar to that of betters, eBay users go online in search of items, bidding on each in an attempt to win the auction. Instead of winning money, eBay-ers win what they have successfully bid on. They will spend money they don't have on items they don't really need but the thrill of winning keeps them coming back for more.

Based upon a traditional Dutch auction, eBay-ers bid on items against other eBay-ers. Items are posted, usually with a closing time for the auction. An eBay-er can view other bids and keep tabs on the auction's progress and price. Addicted buyers go online at all hours, tracking their item in the hopes of placing the winning bid just before the closing deadline. Again, the amount of time and energy invested in this activity is so unbalanced that it can begin to affect the bidder's everyday life.

For the online auction addict, winning provides a feeling of exhilaration, a sense of excitement and a genuine thrill. This "thrill of victory" reinforces the bidder's compulsion to buy the next coveted possession, whether it is a collectible, an antique, a new car or some dubious piece of memorabilia.

By no means is eBay the only online auction house, but it is the largest auction house on the Web. When does legitimate need or simple experimentation with the auction process cross the line and become an addiction? Several common warning signs that a person is addicted to eBay or other auction houses include:

- the need to bid with increasing amounts of money in order to achieve the desired excitement;
- preoccupation with auction houses (thinking about being online when offline, anticipating the next online session or obsessing over the next purchase);
- lying to friends and family members to conceal the extent and nature of his online bidding;
- feeling restless or irritable when attempting to cut down or stop online bidding;
- making repeated unsuccessful efforts to control, cut back or stop online bidding;
- using auction houses as a way of escaping from problems or relieving feelings of helplessness, guilt, anxiety, depression or deprivation;
- jeopardizing or losing a significant relationship, job or educational or career opportunity because of online bidding;
- committing illegal acts such as forgery, fraud, theft or embezzlement to finance bidding activities.

As we have shown, an addiction to auction houses can result in serious personal and financial problems. If this sounds like you or someone you love, consider how eBay or other online auction houses have impacted your life. Has spending gone out of control? Has your need to bid on items taken a toll on your personal life and financial well-being?

OTHER POTENTIAL ONLINE ADDICTIONS

Finally, we want to say a few things about other types of compulsive online behavior. Online shopping, surfing for information or even e-mail can all turn into subtypes of Internet addiction as can any number of other online activities. These are broader in scope and harder to define and determine, but generally the same principles apply. When undue and excessive time, resources and energy are invested in any online activity and when that activity begins to have an impact on a person's relationships, family life or job, Internet abuse has begun. When the Internet user can no longer control or stop his online activity despite its detrimental effects and his desire to quit, the user has become addicted to the Net.

Internet addiction is a multifaceted disorder, with different aspects of the Internet affecting people in different ways. However, the element of escape consistently runs through each type of online abuse. In the following chapter we explore how people become hooked and how the disorder progresses as users become immersed in a virtual fantasy world that takes over their lives and starts to alter how they view and live their reality.

PRAYER CONNECTIONS

"Blessed are the poor in spirit, for theirs is the kingdom of heaven" (Matthew 5:3). In this section of the Gospel of Matthew, Jesus is speaking about attitudes and behaviors that characterize the life of a Christian. This particular beatitude addresses the disciple's relationship with material and nonmaterial goods and possessions. It is not an injunction against *owning* anything but rather a call to gospel stewardship for all things entrusted to our care. When wealth or the acquisition of possessions become the focal point of a Christian's life, it is difficult, if not impossible, to place our time, talents and treasures at the service of others. "For where your treasure is, there your heart will be also" (Matthew 6:21).

CHAPTER SUMMARY QUESTIONS

In Franciscan spirituality poverty of spirit leads to simplicity of life and gratitude. A grateful stance toward life keeps us humble and aware that all is gift. Spend some time reflecting on and writing your responses to the following questions.

1. In what ways is your life simple and uncluttered? Where is the excess and clutter in your life? What is the first step that you can take to make your life simple? How would taking that step affect your day-to-day activities?

2. What are the obstacles that prevent you from being a more responsible steward?

3. Can you identify the many people, things and situations in your current life for which you are or need to be truly grateful? How do

you express that gratitude? When was the last time you consciously thought about your need to be grateful for these gifts?

4. Lack of gratitude often reflects a lack of awareness of the riches we possess; these riches are not all material. Where do you lack awareness or gratitude? If you honestly began to culti-vate simplicity and gratitude in your life on a daily basis, how might this affect your life?

· CHAPTER 3 ·

A State of Hopelessness

My Lord God, I have no idea where I am going. I do not see the
road ahead of me. I cannot know for certain where it will
end. Nor do I really know myself, and the fact that I think
that I am following your will does not mean that I am actu-
ally doing so. But I believe that the desire to please you does
in fact please you. And I hope I have that desire in all that I
am doing. I hope that I will never do anything apart from
that desire. And I know that if I do this you will lead me by
the right road though I may know nothing about it. Therefore
I will trust you always though I may seem to be lost and in
the shadow of death. I will not fear, for you are ever with me,
and you will never leave me to face my perils alone.
—Thomas Merton, *Thoughts on Solitude*[5]

How does Internet addiction grow? It doesn't happen overnight. When people start to use the Internet and realize how much potential it has, they can instantly develop a fascination with it. The wealth of readily available information, the ease with which one can meet new friends and the excitement of finding and keeping in touch with old friends often boggles the mind. It is not unusual for someone just learning Internet skills to be enamored with it and to overindulge time and energy exploring the Web. For some this fascination is not a temporary situation but escalates into an addiction.

In the following pages we explore how Internet use can grow from a simple fascination into a daily habit that can consume a person's time, energy and resources. As a result, an addicted user can damage his marriage, career and personal and spiritual well-being. Eventually, users feel helpless to stop their addictive behavior. This downward spiral often culminates in a state of hopelessness or despair.

THE ADDICTION PROCESS

Internet addiction begins as a normal exploration of the computer and curiosity about all there is to see and do online. The initial discovery of online activities, experiences, content, friends and the potential for streamlining everyday chores opens a doorway into the cyberspace culture. For most people this initial attraction is a temporary event, but for some this typical fascination with the Net begins the addiction process.

As the budding addict becomes comfortable with and begins to trust the technology, he begins to experiment more boldly with the Internet and expands the types of Web sites he visits. The user may access pornography or gambling sites or enter a sex chat room for the very first time. Whatever the behavior or choice of site, it is usually something new or something tempting, and the user would not have tried it if he thought someone were watching.

For those who become hooked, the behavior escalates. They *must* look for new pornography every time they are online; they *must* make another bet at a virtual casino; they *must* enter the chat room and see who else is there. They cross a line from using the Internet as a productive tool to developing a compulsive habit.

Addicted people have incredibly strong urges that impel them to do specific acts. They firmly believe that they need to and must do a specific act in order to survive, and it no longer feels as if they are in control of or responsible for their acts. Most addicts want and try to quit but relapse is only a mouse click away. Their lives become unmanageable as untold hours are spent at the computer; they feel helpless to stop. They drift away from relationships, work responsibilities and family time; they become more isolated as their lives revolve more and more around the computer.

This pattern is common among those who become addicted and can be identified as an addiction process. It has five recognizable stages: discovery, experimentation, escalation, compulsion and hopelessness. The diagram to the right shows the progression of the addictive cycle and how it spirals downward.

These stages of addiction are aptly described as a spiral because the addict visits these stages frequently, each time falling deeper into a more entrenched addiction. The stages are interdependent and highlight how users utilize the Internet as a progressive means of escape. Using online sexual chat rooms as an example of an addictive behavior, each of the stages are described in more detail to illustrate how the addiction cycle grows.

DISCOVERY · EXPERIMENTATION · ESCALATION · COMPULSION · HOPELESSNESS

Stage 1: Discovery

In the early phases of the addiction process, new users feel an excitement associated with the discovery of the Internet. There is so much to see and do online. New users feel thrilled as they first search for information and look at the array of Web sites available on all kinds of subjects. It is an information addict's dream.

The appeal of the Internet is easy to understand. With the press of a button, there is instant access to anything a person wants. She can read her favorite newspapers online; she can search millions of Web sites on her favorite hobbies and interests; she can plan a vacation, make airline reservations and book hotels. It does not take long to discover that the Internet is a powerful tool.

Excitement can be generated by the discovery of online chat rooms, creating an anonymous screen name or handle or clicking onto the Internet as a way to unwind at the end of hard day. This discovery phase makes you want to learn more, see more, do more; it is a never-ending loop. "I was amazed when I first discovered People Connection on AOL," explains Anne, a thirty-nine-year-old bookkeeper from Maine. "I could talk to anyone from anywhere at any time of the day. Even when I was having a bad hair day, I didn't care. The Internet became a constant companion."

Like Anne, many users find it exciting to meet new people online. Early in Kimberly's career, she met a grandmother from Connecticut who became addicted to the Internet. "When I first discovered chat rooms, I was amazed at all the different people I met online. One person was a musician, another was a scuba diver from Florida, and another was a local politician running for reelection as mayor of his town. It opened up a whole new world for me talking with all these people, leading lives certainly more interesting than mine. I was recently widowed, and my children were grown and had moved away. I guess making new friends online filled a void in my life."

Access to chat rooms and interactive online activities can also lead to the discovery of sexually explicit content, such as adult Web sites and sex chat rooms. A man doing research online may accidentally bump into a pornographic Web site. A woman might enter a social chat room and meet a man who entices her to have cybersex with him. The proliferation of sexually explicit material provides an outlet for a curious person's initial exploration.

"The first time I tried cybersex I had no idea what I was getting into," explained Shelia, a forty-one-year-old divorcée from Houston. "I met Mike three months ago in a poetry chat room. We both loved Emerson and Hawthorne, and after three months of flirting it was almost like we were dating. One day the conversation grew sexual. It made me feel so wanted and so attractive, which I hadn't felt in a long time, not since I divorced my husband over four years ago."

PRAYER CONNECTIONS

Catholic writers through the centuries have addressed what happens to those who seek true happiness in anything other than God. Francis Thompson, in the poem "The Hound of Heaven," describes a person's desperate attempts to avoid God, who is "all good, supremely good, totally good,"[6] by immersing himself in a succession of lesser goods, such as nature and knowledge. Centuries earlier Saint Augustine of Hippo wrote "our hearts are restless, O God, until they rest in You."[7] In his *Confessions*, he details his conversion process and elaborates on all the things that absorbed his attention and kept him from peace and from God.

In one of the most beautiful and real prayers ever written, Augustine reflects on his experiences of being lost and absorbed in what does not satisfy. Because he writes from the vantage point of his later years, he can also celebrate and rejoice in his healing.

We invite you to pray with Saint Augustine this prayer that testifies to the power and availability of grace no matter how far we believe we have strayed from God:

> Late have I loved You, O Beauty ever ancient, ever new;
> late have I loved you! You were within me, but I was out-
> side, and it was there that I searched for you. In my
> unloveliness I plunged into the lovely things which you
> created. You were with me, but I was not with you.
> Created things kept me from you; yet if they had not
> been in you they would have not been at all. You called,
> you shouted, and you broke through my deafness. You

> flashed, you shone, and you dispelled my blindness. You
> breathed your fragrance on me; I drew in breath and
> now I pant for you. I have tasted you, now I hunger and
> thirst for more. You touched me, and I burned for your
> peace.[8]

Stage 2: Experimentation

Cyberspace, with its lack of restrictions, opens the door for users to explore new types of sexual behavior. In one study Kimberly conducted, she found that over 60 percent of online users who became addicted to online sex developed their addiction to sex exclusively through the Internet. Individuals who never had a problem with sexual addiction found themselves drawn to online sex, chatting away in adult chat rooms, using voice chat to hear what others had to say about sex, or using Web cams to film and explore voyeuristic and exhibitionistic sexual behavior.

Most people do not yet realize that there is any risk involved in experimenting in online sexual pursuits. While in some ways it may seem like a journey into foreign territory, online sexual behaviors occur in the familiar and comfortable environment of one's home or office. Users feel safe using the computer, which encourages more adventurous and riskier behaviors. A curious person may be completely unprepared when he enters into one of many rooms specifically designed for the purposes of facilitating sexual experimentation.

As we described in the last chapter, behind the anonymity of cyberspace, online users can conceal their age, marital status, gender, race, vocation, education or appearance. Addicts use this anonymity to experiment and explore things online that they would never do in real life, often taking on fictional personas or character roles.

The Internet gateway allows users to secretly begin to experiment online without the fear of being caught. With this newfound sense of freedom, they feel encouraged and validated by the acceptance of others; they achieve a sense of belonging because they are now members of the cyberspace culture; they feel less accountable for their actions over the Internet. When coupled with the idea that this behavior is OK because it is not *really* happening, powerful reinforcement occurs and can cause the delusion that this behavior is justifiable.

Within the anonymous context of cyberspace, conventional messages about sex are eliminated, thus allowing users to play out hidden or repressed sexual fantasies in a private lab. Furthermore, since online experiences often occur in the privacy of one's home, office or bedroom, they facilitate the perception of anonymity and that Internet use is personal and untraceable. For anyone who has ever been curious about a particular fantasy, cyberspace offers an anonymous way to explore and indulge in those fantasies.

Stage 3: Escalation

As the drug addict or alcoholic requires larger and larger doses of the drug to achieve the same sensation and pleasure from the experience, the Internet addict becomes bored with routine fantasies and now looks for the next big virtual thrill. In the escalation stage, the behavior becomes more chronic and pronounced: The addict becomes saturated with a continuous stream of sexual content that usually devolves into riskier and riskier forms.

Given that the addict lacks proper impulse control, he may be more likely to dabble in sexually inappropriate or deviant material, which is easily accessible on the Internet. This is especially troublesome when the addict experiments in pedophilic or incest themed chat rooms, which abound in cyberspace. While these are branded as "fantasy only" chat rooms, it is difficult to decipher what is fact and what is fantasy based upon the chat dialogues. Therefore, it is unclear from the discussion if users are describing fictional stories, sexual fantasies, stories about past activities or plans for the future.

In many respects, it is easy to understand the allure of cyber-sex when a person can be anyone, say anything and no one else will know. The make-believe online sexual adventure is independent of reality, and it doesn't matter if a cyber-lover is really telling the truth or just pretending. The sexual satisfaction and intensity can still be very potent and exhilarating.

In order to deal with the double-life that occurs, the addict often rationalizes the behavior and disowns what he says or does online with self-statements such as, "It's just a fantasy," or "This isn't who I really am." Addicts detach from the online experience and perceive their secret fantasy world as a parallel life that is completely separate from who they are in real life. However, these rationalizations are temporary and eventually break down as the addict becomes more and more disgusted by his online actions and experiences episodes of despair as promises to stop are broken and attempts to quit fail.

PRAYER CONNECTIONS

In the book of Genesis, Scripture reveals the most basic fact about human beings: We are created in the image of God (cf. 1:26). God is Unity, and when humans compartmentalize their lives, they fall into a state of *dis*-ease and *dis*-harmony. Life is out of sync—and it shows. All the lies we tell ourselves do not change the fact that something is seriously wrong, and try as we might, we can never fully escape that fact.

For anyone caught in stages two or three of Internet addiction or for anyone hoping such a person will come to grips with the ever-emerging and growing problem, we encourage you to make a mantra (a short, often repeated phrase) of the following words from Psalm 139:1, 3.

> O LORD, you have searched me and known me…
> and are acquainted with all my ways.

Repeat these words often and think of their meaning in light of what we perceive to be "secret behavior."

In a spiritual direction session, Patrice led a woman with an Internet addiction through a guided meditation. The woman visualized Jesus walking into the room while she was online and asking, "What are you doing?" Hold that conversation with Jesus, then write the words from Psalm 139 on paper and tape it across the computer screen.

Stage 4: Compulsivity

As behavior escalates, online use becomes more chronic and more ingrained and develops into a full-blown compulsive obsession. In this stage life becomes unmanageable for the addict as relationships or careers are jeopardized and even ruined because of the compulsive behavior.

In this stage the addict is largely driven by increasingly painful states of tension and agitation, as an alcoholic is driven to drink at moments of excessive stress or an overeater is driven to binge on food during moments of tension. The addict becomes preoccupied with the computer and constantly feels a longing to be online whenever offline. The addict attempts to conceal the nature of her online activities and fears that others will discover her secret online life. Realizing the impact of this destructive pattern, the addict tries to rationalize the behavior and continues to engage in the activity despite its known potential risks, including possible job loss, divorce or arrest.

In one such case a thirty-four-year-old minister arrested for possession of child pornography obtained from the Internet explained, "I soon discovered the vast array of pornography, including child pornography, available on the Internet. My attraction to pornography on the computer was born of sheer amazement at the volume of available material, and this amazement turned to fascination and ultimately to obsession. I knew it was wrong to look at this material. My life became a lonely, isolated mess. I realized that I could lose my job, my marriage and the respect of everyone I love if I were caught. I have two daughters and would never think about doing anything inappropriate with them, but I could not bring myself to stop despite knowing all the consequences of my actions."

For the addict, what she does online becomes a source of nurturing, the focus of energy and an origin of excitement. The online experience turns into a relief from pain and anxiety, a reward for success and a way to avoid addressing other emotional issues in the person's life. The addiction is truly an altered state of consciousness in which "normal" behavior pales by comparison in terms of excitement and relief from troubles that are associated with the Internet. In this way, the online world becomes a private refuge as the addict displays a progressive retreat into the computer as a means to avoid life's complications and responsibilities.

Stage 5: Hopelessness

In the final stage of the addiction process, the addict hits that metaphorical rock bottom only to realize the extent of the damage caused by his addiction. Feelings of hopelessness and helplessness develop, especially as the addict becomes fully aware of how out of control life has become because of the Internet. In this stage the addict realizes the unhealthy excess of the behavior only to attempt total abstinence. They will often cancel their Internet service, disconnect the modems or install filtering software in an attempt to stop the compulsive behavior. The addict struggles with staying clean and sober and feels desperate to put his life back on track. Since relapse is only a mouse click away, the addict usually slips back into old patterns and begins the cycle once again.

"I know my addiction to online pornography is destroying my marriage. We are now sleeping in separate beds, and I am alone all night with my computer instead of her. I know this is sick. I want to quit doing this, but I just feel too weak to stop."

In the hopelessness stage the addict experiences a period of deep regret after the online experience. The addict engages in denigrating negative thoughts about himself that only serve to reinforce the despair. Self-statements such as: "I am helpless because I can't control my use," "I am weak," "I am defective," and "I am disgusting because of my dirty online habit" only add to the person's misery. The addict views the behavior as a personal failure and may be profoundly distressed that those he loves are suffering as a result of his uncontrollable behavior.

At this point most addicts begin a merry-go-round ride of promising to quit, succeeding briefly and then reengaging in the behavior. During the intervals of abstinence the addict temporarily engages in healthy patterns of behavior, resumes interests in old hobbies, spends more time with her family, exercises and gets enough rest. However, during stressful or emotionally charged moments the addict feels tempted to return to the computer and begins to crave the Internet. Addicts try to justify their need to go online and rationalize, "Just a few minutes won't hurt," or "I can control my Internet use." Addicts tell themselves that the Internet is the best way to relax and feel good about themselves, and they begin not to care about the consequences. They remember how good being online felt, and they forget how badly they felt afterward. The addict breaks down, gives into the urge, and the cycle repeats itself. Feelings of hopelessness intensify after the relapse, and the addict despairs that she can ever stop.

At this stage an addict is very emotionally vulnerable and his life may begin to disintegrate. Those he loves and who have tried to support him in making healthy choices may realize that they can no longer provide a safety net for him. Previously understanding bosses have to face their bottom line and so fire the addict for lack of productivity. At this point some addicts are depressed enough to commit suicide.

In some ways a person caught in stages four and five who has a faith or spiritual background has an even more difficult time coping with the addiction. Added to all the other layers of pain and distress is a sense of having failed God and the fear of condemnation. The person convinces herself that she is beyond saving and even beyond God's healing reach. All the discourse and reassuring Scripture in the world cannot convince her otherwise.

At this point a person is embroiled in an emotional morass. She cannot trust her feelings; she may be numb to anything other than her pain and the thrill of satisfying her addiction. Feeling only pain or thrill sounds like an oxymoron, but it demonstrates just how emotionally tangled the person has become. Because Scripture so often appeals to the heart, the addict may not be able to access its wisdom and may even be angry that someone has suggested such a "simple" solution.

When the windows to the emotions are so fully blocked, sometimes the doorway is logic and reason. Reminding a person of faith about the church's teaching on moral blame and sin may be helpful. The church has consistently taught that the commission of serious sin requires three conditions that must be present at the time the act is performed:

1. The matter must be serious or considered serious.
2. The person must intend the evil.
3. The person must freely choose to do the evil.

In the case of an addiction, especially an addiction that is having such a disruptive impact on a person's life and the lives of those he loves, condition one is solidly met. When we begin to explore an addict's intention, we move to shakier ground. An addict, especially one under stress, feels compelled to spend time at the computer and access material online, but does he actually intend to initiate the self-defeating behavior and its full range of consequences? The answer to this question cannot be found in any book and must be answered by the only person who can determine the truth—the addict himself.

With regard to the third condition concerning freedom, most moral theologians and professionals who counsel addicted persons would agree that an addiction, by its very nature, places severe limits on a person's ability to make free choices. This does not mean that one must condone or tolerate the behavior, but it does speak about how much moral responsibility the addict may bear for his behaviors.

Patrice was counseling Tom, a young man who had attended Catholic grade school, high school and college. He had a severe addiction to buying Civil War memorabilia online. He had reached the point which he was about to lose his home (there was a lien on the house), and his wife did not know what was going on. Tom's despair was palpable, and he voiced his fear that "this sin puts me beyond God." Patrice reminded Tom about the teachings mentioned above. At his next session Tom stated that he had thought much about what was said and for the first time in a very long time, allowed himself to think that there might be hope—and help.

Some people get nervous or angry when they read about this church teaching in a book on addiction. They often feel that *the one who is responsible* for all this mess is getting off scot-free. They look around and see that their lives are in chaos as a result of the other's addiction and want to hold that person accountable. They also want God to hold the person accountable. This too is part of the healing process; the painful feelings must be acknowledged and worked through.

PRAYER CONNECTIONS

The Serenity Prayer has led and sustained millions of addicted people and the ones who have loved them on their journey to recovery. As you pray this prayer, think about all the people who have prayed it through the years, the cumulative depth of addiction that it has addressed and the untold numbers who employ it as a vital tool in their recovery process.

> Lord, grant me the serenity to accept the things
> I cannot change,
> the courage to change the things I can,
> and the wisdom to know the difference.

CHAPTER 4

Who Is Most at Risk?

While it may appear that addictions are pleasure-seeking behaviors, the roots of any addiction can usually be traced to a wish to suppress or avoid some kind of emotional pain. Addiction is a way to escape from reality, from something that is either too full of sadness (such as an abusive relationship) or too devoid of joy (an emotionally empty life). Emotional trauma in early life may also be the source of many addictions.

Internet addiction offers a fantasy world in which there are endless people who appear to be interesting to—and interested in—the person. Young, socially awkward or emotionally troubled individuals may find it easier to engage in Internet "relationships" than risk the face-to-face rejection of a real person. As an addict becomes more immersed in this shadow world, denial takes hold and she comes to view these "friends" and "partners" as more real than an actual spouse or family member.

As the addiction cycle grows, the Internet becomes a way for the addict to self-medicate in order to temporarily run away from life's problems. Over time, however, this coping mechanism proves to be unproductive and potentially harmful as the issues hidden by the addictive behavior culminate in larger and larger problems. While not everyone becomes addicted to the Internet in the same way for the same reason, some general patterns have emerged as to why people become hooked and the ways in which they use the Internet to escape from or cope with underlying problems in their lives.

A SUBSTITUTE FOR RELATIONSHIPS AND INTIMACY

Internet addicts have difficulty forming intimate relationships with others and hide behind the anonymity of cyberspace to connect with others in a nonthreatening way. Online a person can create a social network of new relationships. With routine visits to a particular group (for example, a specific chat area, MUD or news group), a person can establish a high degree of familiarity with other group members, thus creating a sense of community. Like all communities, the cyberspace culture has its own set of values, standards, language, signs and artifacts. Individual users adapt to the current norms of the group. Existing solely online, the group often disregards normal conventions about privacy (e.g., by posting personal messages to public bulletin boards or chat rooms); it exists in a parallel time and space and is kept alive only by users connecting with one another via the computer.

Once membership into a particular group has been established, Internet addicts rely upon the conversation exchange for companionship, advice, understanding and even romance. The ability to create a virtual community leaves the physical world behind to the degree that well-known, fixed and actual people no longer exist, and anonymous online users form a meeting of the minds living in a purely text-based society. Through the exchange of online messages, users find deep psychological meaning and connection, quickly form intimate bonds and feel emotionally close to others.

In cyberspace all social conventions regarding politeness are gone. Personal questions about one's marital status, age, financial status or weight may be, and sometimes are expected to be, asked upon an initial virtual meeting. The immediacy of such open and personal information about oneself fosters a sense of intimacy among others in the online community at a rate that rarely occurs in real life. After just one online exchange, a user may reveal to a complete stranger details about his personal life, and this intimate sharing creates a close bond in the mind of the speaker; it also engenders feelings of closeness, acceptance and belonging. This immediate exchange of personal information also opens the way for becoming involved in the lives of others whom they have never met. In some ways the experience is like watching a soap opera on television: The addict becomes totally immersed in and concerned about the lives of characters that do not exist in reality.

"I was thirty-seven and disabled," explained one man. "I fell at work carrying a stack of water bottles for the purification company that I worked for. I'd been home and in pain for the past three years. I lived alone and didn't know much about computers. I went online at first to look for information on pain relief and found a support group online. I was chatting with other folks who understood what I was going through. I never made close friends, but I talked about personal things with these people. I told them about the accident, my divorce, being a drunk for the first year I was on disability. I told them everything—things I never told people before and nothing I would tell anyone again."

The formation of such virtual arenas creates a group dynamic of social support to answer a deep and compelling need in people whose real lives are interpersonally impoverished and devoid of intimacy. Some circumstances, such as being a home-bound caretaker, disabled person, retired individual or home-maker, can limit a person's access to others. In these cases individuals are more likely to use the Internet as an alternative means to develop the social foundations that are lacking in their immediate environments. In other cases, those who feel socially awkward or who have difficulty developing healthy relationships in real life find that they are able to express themselves more freely, form close relationships with others and find the companionship and acceptance missing in their lives. These are powerful reinforcements that impel a user to return again and again to the source of affirmation.

A HINT OF SELF-ESTEEM AND SELF-CONFIDENCE

Internet addicts often feel tense, lonely, restless, depressed, withdrawn, angry or worthless and use cyberspace to wash away these feelings and temporarily feel confident, well-liked, proud or in love. As users become more involved in their virtual relationships, individuals are able to take more emotional risks by voicing controversial opinions about religion, abortion or other value-laden issues. In real life Internet addicts are often afraid to express their opinions even to their closest confidants or their spouses. However, in cyberspace they feel free to risk exposing their true feelings without fear of rejection, confrontation or judgment since they can keep their identities well masked.

For example, a priest who was active and well respected in his parish disagreed with aspects of the Catholic faith, such as not allowing women to be priests and mandatory celibacy. Yet he would never voice his reservations about the Catholic faith publicly to his congregation. He kept his views to himself until he discovered a discussion group for former Catholics; here he openly voiced his opinions without fear of retribution.

Beyond the airing of deep-rooted feelings, the Internet allows the exchange of positive and negative feedback elicited from a quorum of other users. Those who shared his views comforted the priest, and those who challenged him provided a dialogue to debate such issues without him having to reveal his vocation or true identity.

In this way people take on character roles when they interact with others online. They feel that they "become" another person. Online each user has the ability to remove the imposed constraints of real life in order to experiment with altered perceptions of self. That is, cyberspace creates a virtual "stage" where a person can act in a new role through the creation of fictitious handles and the projection of altered physical characteristics such as gender, age, race or family background. This inaccurate description of self cultivates a persona or false image of oneself, allowing a person to "reconstruct" her identity.

Creating a persona through a fictitious handle allows one to mentally transform herself into a new person online. Most times an online persona is a paradox of one's real life, a purely text-based identity that is qualitatively different from the physical world. Socioeconomic status, gender, age and race all play a role in the development of a person's identity, and it is from this sense of self that humans build the basis for all interpersonal interactions. In cyberspace such issues fade into the background because all virtual inhabitants are created equal. This equality fosters confidence when interacting within social environments online. However, virtually acquired social skills do not transfer to real-life relationships with their constant ebb and flow of inequality. Therefore, such text-based identities—with all their competencies and skills—appear to be firmly planted inside the computer screen and trapped in cyberspace.

One gentleman, a fifty-year-old construction worker who described having a "good life" with his wife and kids, emerged online as "Lucky," a rich entrepreneur. After his forays into the "Millionaires' Lounge" chat room, he realized that he lacked the achievement and recognition he wanted in real life. "It didn't occur to me until I pretended to be someone else online, but when I look back, I wish I were more successful and financially secure." Lucky found it exciting to be able to step away from all his responsibilities as husband, father and provider and become a completely different person online. His mental absorption in the new role that had nothing to do with his real life was a form of relaxation, just like going to the movies, watching television or playing a video game. Such amusements allow the mind to take a vacation from the stress and demands of the roles we play in real life. The Internet serves the same purpose as these more traditional types of stress relief. The added attraction is that the Net also provides instant feedback about the persona that is projected, and one is able to gauge others' responses to it without having to use or develop relationship skills. The difficulty is that while online relationships may meet a need in the here-and-now, they do little, if anything, to resolve issues or prepare one for future encounters with real people.

Individuals who suffer from low self-esteem, who feel lonely, restless or withdrawn can use cyberspace connections with others to feel better about themselves and their circumstances. One woman explained, "At forty-five I still lived alone and was so shy that I had trouble with any kind of relationship. Weekends were the hardest to get through. Friday nights I rented a movie; Saturdays I did errands; and every Sunday my mother called to see if I had a man in my life. It was a constant reminder of how empty my life was." Through the Internet she began meeting men on Match.com and had several Internet dates. She was spending nearly every weekend on the computer. When online, she felt like a new woman. She was outgoing, confident and felt a renewed purpose.

"It was a complete transformation," she said. "My handle, Unbridled Lady, brought out a whole new side of me. It was exciting to create a new version of myself online. I had friends, I greeted everyone who entered the chat room, and I even fell in love. He is divorced and wants to meet. My life that once had no direction now seems complete, and every time I go online, I feel good about myself and where I am in life."

Online people can experience a rebirth, finding a safe outlet to express hidden feelings or a place to discover new aspects of their personality. When people feel down, troubled or lonely, the Internet becomes an instant source of new relationships, companionship and understanding; it offers a way for them to feel better about themselves.

PRAYER CONNECTIONS

You will need a journal and pen for this reflection. In all likelihood, you will need to work on this exercise over a period of time. You may need to spend several sessions on just one section before you have a sense of having finished it. Take as much time as you need. For each session, repeat steps one, two, three and eight. If at any time, you begin to feel overwhelmed, distraught or too emotionally vulnerable, stop what you are doing and try again later. If you cannot resume this exercise with some level of emotional balance, seriously consider finding a spiritual director, counselor or therapist who can help you work through it because you have probably tapped into one of the core issues that needs to be resolved and healed.

1. Find a quiet, private space where you can be alone, comfortable and uninterrupted for at least thirty to sixty minutes.

2. Remind yourself that you are a child of God. No matter what is going on in your life at this time, this does not change.

3. Recall a Gospel story about Jesus interacting with the people around him and pay attention to his compassion, understanding and willingness to help. Ask Jesus to be with you in the same way as you work on this exercise.

4. Remember your earliest memory of a relationship problem—it may have been being teased, being punished, being left out. Write what happened in your journal.

5. Remember how you felt as a result of this situation. Get in touch with those feelings and name them in your journal.

6. What were the messages you told yourself—then and now—as a result of this experience? What are or were the flaws in your perception? How have these erroneous messages affected your life? Journal your responses.

7. Invite Jesus to share the messages he wants you to hear as a result of this painful experience. Remain quiet and attentive and write down any thoughts or statements that come to mind.

8. When you are ready, pray a closing prayer and leave your quiet place.

9. Read what you have written at least once a day for three days; go back to it as you feel led; write down any additional thoughts or feelings.

AN EMOTIONAL RELEASE AND CATHARSIS

Internet addicts tend to suffer from depression, anxiety and emotional problems and use the Internet to fulfill unmet needs or to act out repressed feelings. Those who suffer from low self-esteem, feelings of inadequacy or frequent disapproval from others are at the highest risk for developing a secret online identity. The negative self-concepts that addicts subscribe to usually lead to clinical problems of depression and anxiety, which may also be intertwined with excessive online use and elaborate, grandiose self-presentations. This "ideal self" becomes a secret life carried out in the anonymous surroundings of cyberspace.

The creation of a pseudo-identity allows a person to enjoy a secret life, a life that blocks out unpleasant thoughts about self and one's real situation. The online identity masks interpersonal insecurity and cultivates a fantasy life that satisfies a personal wish fulfillment. By investing so much time and energy into the secret life, a person is able to meet previously unmet psychological needs.

Personas also offer individuals an outlet to access different parts of their personality, thus allowing an individual to expand the range of emotions experienced and expressed toward others. Psychoanalytic theory examines repressed parts of one's personality that are experienced on unconscious levels; these sometimes reveal themselves in slips of the tongue or dreams. In this context, Sigmund Freud points out that our unconscious motives drive human behavior yet remain largely outside our awareness.[9]

Internet addicts feel a sense of being able to unlock parts of themselves—parts that have been repressed in their real lives—through creating online personas. The ability to unlock repressed aspects of the self can take on various forms. In cyberspace a shy person can become outgoing, a nonsexual person can be sexual, a nonassertive person can be forceful, or an aloof person can be gregarious. Some online users experience their online personas as a way of coping or struggling through repressed feelings such as anger with a parent, anger with a spouse or anger at a child. Cyberspace then becomes a place to play out parts of themselves that they fear or consciously avoid confronting in real life.

For example, Tony, married for three years and the father of an eighteen-month-old daughter, became addicted to *Doom II* on a local bulletin board system. He said, "By day I am a mild-mannered husband, but at night I become the most aggressive jerk online."

Tony had always been a loner. He described how growing up

as the middle child, he felt ignored by his parents. He had built up a great deal of resentment toward his siblings and hated his parents for his perceived neglect. On the outside they always looked like the perfect family, but no one knew of the anger and resentment that he felt inside.

Tony was afraid to give into his anger, yet in cyberspace he overcame his fear and dominated others, becoming one of the most aggressive players in the game.

"I could beat up other players, kill monsters, slay dragons, continually releasing all my pent-up aggression," Tony explained. He believed that this emotional outlet was not only exciting but also filled an emotional void. As he described, "I became another person who was everything I wasn't in real life. I became so fixed on being a good little boy for my parents that I stifled all my other emotions." By unleashing this repressed part of himself, Tony believed that he maintained better emotional balance and prevented explosive outbursts directed at his wife, boss or daughter. Through Tony's online experience, he was able to find a safe outlet to express his anger in the form of a character in this virtual role-playing game.

As so many Internet addicts learn, what is awakened emotionally through the emergence of repressed aspects of the self is difficult to stuff back into the unconscious. Once this material is open to the conscious, one must deal with its aftereffects. Of paramount importance is learning to embrace these aspects of self and integrate them in a healthy manner into one's true personality. Otherwise, one risks living a very compartmentalized or split life, and wholeness and balance are not found in either the everyday world or the world of cyberspace. In Tony's case his aggressive personality and resentment were totally relegated to cyberspace, and he resumed his "good little boy" role of being a good husband and father when he clicked offline.

The dichotomy was too painful, and soon he became so absorbed in his *Doom* role that he neglected his family. He could not tolerate disruptions when he was online. He came to resent his wife for asking him to take time away from the Internet, much as he had silently resented his siblings. Tony snapped when she needed attention and felt angry when she wanted him to help with their child. The awakening of his repressed feelings undermined the quality of his family life. Now that he had unlocked his repressed aggressive side, he didn't know how to suppress it again, nor did he know how to tame it so that he could effectively channel it into his real life relationships.

MULTIPLE ADDICTIONS

Internet addicts often suffer from multiple addictions. This is defined as a combination of two or more addictions coexisting in the same person. At any given time one or more of the addictions, such as overeating, smoking, alcoholism, drug use, sex addiction or compulsive gambling may become the addiction of the moment. At other times the various addictions will function simultaneously. This layering of addictions is an extension of underlying compulsive tendencies.

Addiction counselors often talk about people who suffer from a "compulsive personality" or individuals who do everything to excess. These are the people who drink too much, smoke too much, eat too much, shop too much or drink too much caffeine. Compulsive personalities have trouble controlling their intake of substances such as alcohol, nicotine, food or caffeine, or may be individuals who feel compelled to eat or shop at every moment of stress and tension in their lives. We explained earlier how process addictions act as a mental escape for addicts, and the substance or behavior of choice isn't as important as looking at what is driving the addiction.

For people who already suffer from compulsive gambling, sexual behavior or shopping behavior, the Internet serves as a new outlet to engage in these addictions. Gambling addicts find virtual casinos to be a new venue for gambling; sex addicts discover a new source for sexual gratification through online pornography and anonymous sex chat; shopping addicts browse the new marketplace of online shopping sites.

New addictions can also emerge. People can develop addictions to online gaming, chat rooms, instant messaging, blogging (posting personal writing online), downloading music or Web surfing. For those in recovery from other addictions, the Internet allows them to continue compulsive behaviors, giving the addict something new to lean on when feeling worried or troubled. Recovering addicts often struggle with how to overcome difficult situations or emotional problems while abstaining from alcohol, drugs, sex or food. They miss the escape hatch their addictions provided and while learning to live without them, they may turn to the Internet as a new and socially acceptable way to cope. What they don't realize is that by doing so they have perpetuated the addictive cycle.

One woman explained, "I had been a recovering alcoholic for two years. One day my sponsor told me about online Alcoholics Anonymous meetings, which I started to use in between my real-life AA meetings. I didn't think I'd get so hooked. Every time I felt like drinking, I turned to the Net. I would get depressed or down about something and to keep me sober from the booze, I guess I fell into the Internet. When I was online, I didn't have to deal with the pain or emotions associated with my divorce and the loss of my job because of drinking. The Internet became a substitute for alcohol and kept me from moving on and rebuilding my life."

Addicts in recovery from some addiction often look to the Internet as a way to escape reality without really dealing with the underlying problems that cause the addictive behavior. When an addict abstains from his addiction, he loses the emotional safety net that the dependency provided. As a result, the stress that comes from a job, marriage or relationships in general can trigger addictive online behavior. Using the Internet becomes a quick fix and an instant cure that washes away troubling feelings, feelings that they have never learned to deal with. Recovering addicts who feel overwhelmed or who experience work problems or money problems or who experience life-changing events such as divorce, relocation or a death in the family can become easily absorbed in a virtual world full of fantasy and intrigue. Online they can lose themselves in anything that piques their interest, and the problems and difficulties of their lives fade into the background as their attention becomes completely focused on the Internet.

AN ARENA FOR SEXUAL EXPLORATION

Internet addicts and in particular online sex addicts perceive their own sexual needs as immoral or deviant and use cybersex to validate their sexual urges. Sex is such an important part of being human, but for most, sex is rarely discussed openly in a positive manner. Our families may have said very little, if anything, about the intimacy, power and sacredness of sex around the nightly dinner table. For the most part, we learned about sex from friends, books or school health class long before our parents even thought to talk with us about it. If our parents did talk about sex with us, they may have been uncomfortable or embarrassed, sending us implicit messages that engaging in sex was somehow naughty or shameful, even at its best. In this environment, we keep our questions to ourselves and wonder if we are normal.

Cybersex changes all that. Instead of sex being hidden in adult bookstores located on the outskirts of town, cyberspace provides one with the opportunity to freely explore all things sexual without fear of discovery. It also offers a forum for honestly expressing one's sexual questions and fantasies. When these sexual thoughts receive acceptance and affirmation online, it helps the cybersex user normalize her sexual feelings. The problem with this is that every sexual idea and fantasy can find validation on the Web, no matter how deviant or bizarre.

The variety and scope of computer-enabled fantasies are limitless and still evolving. In the post-Internet era, new chat rooms, new technology and new online users all help to build new sexual-fantasy experiences. Given this variety, users can tap into new sexual identities, unlocking hidden or repressed sexual feelings.

Nancy, a fifty-two-year-old nurse, discovered cybersex five months ago. She routinely went to sex chat rooms and met different men for casual cybersex. While Nancy found it all fun at first, she eventually became bored with the same routine, so she decided to try out different types of sex chat rooms to add some excitement. While Nancy was enjoying her new sexual freedom online, her work suffered. She started coming in late, leaving early and calling in sick just to stay home and chat. Her habit became an obsession.

Before the Internet obsession Nancy had been married to Hank for almost twenty-five years, and they had three grown children and one grandchild. By her own definition she had led a normal life and had never thought deeply about her fantasies until she discovered sex on the Internet. "Through the Internet I no longer felt like a bad or immoral person for having these feelings and finally felt sexually connected and liberated. The trouble is that I no longer wanted sex with my husband. It was killing everything—my work, my marriage, my family life—but I felt helpless to stop."

PRAYER CONNECTIONS

If the stories of the men and women you have read about in this book seem all too familiar to you, then either you or someone you love is struggling with an Internet addiction. In the midst of the chaos that any addiction brings to a relationship or family, it is good to have some reminders that there are indeed truths on which we can depend—no matter how hopeless life seems. The following words from Scripture can be prayed often throughout the day as an affirmation or as a sign of one's hope or faith in God. Choose the ones that speak to you, copy them and repeat them often. You may find it helpful to read the entire psalm or passage from which the verse is taken.

Even though I walk through the darkest valley,
   I fear no evil;
for you are with me. (Psalm 23:4)

God is our refuge and strength,
   a very present help in trouble. (Psalm 46:1)

Create in me a clean heart, O God,
   and put a new and right spirit within me. (Psalm 51:10)

[A] broken and contrite heart,
      O God, you will not despise. (Psalm 51:17)

Restore us, O God;
   let your face shine, that we may be saved. (Psalm 80:3)

Incline your ear, O LORD, and answer me,
   for I am poor and needy. (Psalm 86:1)

Bless the LORD, O my soul,
   and do not forget all his benefits—
who forgives all your iniquity,
   who heals all your diseases. (Psalm 103:2–3)

I have gone astray like a lost sheep;
      seek out your servant. (Psalm 119:176)

Out of the depths I cry to you, O LORD.
   Lord, hear my voice! (Psalm 130:1–2)

Cast all your anxiety on [God], because he cares for you.
(1 Peter 5:7)

· CHAPTER 5 ·

Internet Addiction: Undermining the Marriage Relationship

Therefore what God has joined together, let no one separate.
—Matthew 19:6

We know from a long history of documented studies that many marriages become vulnerable during times of crisis. How often we read in the paper or hear on the news that a couple who has recently endured some form of trauma has separated or divorced. The stress and pain generated by the situation proves too much for the couple to cope with or resolve. Even though a long history of documented studies examining the effects of Internet addiction on marriage does not yet exist, counselors and ministers are already seeing a pattern of disturbing results.

Any serious addiction has the potential to drive a wedge between couples. Online addictions are no different; in fact, some unique characteristics of Internet addiction, particularly the ability to remain anonymous, the illusion of privacy and secrecy and its ready availability, increase the risk factors.

WARNING: ONLINE ADDICTIONS ARE DANGEROUS TO YOUR MARRIAGE
In this section we are going to examine two examples of specific Internet addictions and show how their presence in a spouse can affect a marriage. Compulsive online gambling or shopping has an impact on a couple's financial stability. In the extreme these addictions can jeopardize a couple's ability to provide adequately for themselves and a family. People have lost homes, cars, savings and credit ratings because of debt incurred through these pursuits. Perhaps even more significant, they lose trust in their partner and see the collapse of dreams. As bills pile up, their hopes for the future often go down the drain. Money that was saved or set aside to take a once-in-a-lifetime vacation or to ease the strain on finances that even predictable expenses can create disappears in the black hole of addiction.

Josh came to counseling when all his attempts to curb his wife's online shopping addiction failed. He'd cut up credit cards, emptied joint bank accounts and shut off Internet service at home. Unfortunately, there are unscrupulous businesses that cater to people desperate for money—regardless of the reason. His wife Betty found such places and incurred even larger debts because of outrageous interest rates on her loans. Josh was feeling completely overwhelmed. Betty was spending far more than they could reasonably be expected to cover, and her income was decreasing because she was taking unpaid days off to indulge in the addiction. Josh was deeply concerned about the couple's ability to maintain their home; he also worried about the impact of budgetary constraints on their three school-age children.

"I love my wife and wish I knew how to help her. But I have my kids to think about, too. I don't know how long they'll be able to stay in Catholic school—the last tuition payment went to buy some expensive luggage that we needed like we need a hole in the head. I don't know what to do. The thought of leaving Betty tears me apart, but as long as we're legally married, I'm responsible for her debts, and she's putting the kids at risk. Her solution is to buy lottery tickets because, she says, 'I just know I'm going to hit it big, and then you won't have to worry.' She's totally out of touch with reality, and I don't know how much more I can or should take."

As of this writing, Josh was still looking for ways to maintain his marriage and unilaterally reduce their debt. But like so many couples in this situation, he was running out of options and knew the day was soon coming when he would have to make a choice between preserving his marriage and providing stability for his children. Betty was still in denial about the extent of her addiction and the consequences it was having on her family.

It is true that the Internet has created jobs and some people have made viable careers from selling items on shopping or auction sites. The key word here is "viable." These people have found ways to maintain appropriate boundaries between work and home: They have a work schedule, usually with flexible hours; they devote time to home and family; others can recognize their endeavors as a legitimate business. The compulsive seller does not have these protective boundaries in his place, and his "work" permeates every aspect of his life.

As far-fetched as it may seem, online game playing fits into this category. There are legitimate uses for interactive online games. When used in moderation, these games can help overcome stress, boredom and loneliness; they can provide a safe release for anger; they can even help ward off or alleviate depression. However, when game playing consistently and increasingly usurps time and attention that needs to be directed elsewhere, healthy boundaries are destroyed and the door to addiction is opened.

When a spouse is so absorbed in an online activity that there is no time or attention left over to nurture a marriage or family, relationships are compromised. Because online addictions can be yielded to in so many different venues and the computer can be such an integral part of a person's work, the spouse of a person addicted to online activity often lives in fear of its consequences. Even when the addicted spouse is at home, there is no guarantee that she will not indulge in the compulsive behavior, even to the exclusion or ignoring of children, family obligations or routine tasks. If children are involved, the nonaddicted spouse worries about the example that is being set as well as the parent-child relationship. In the case of severe addiction, a spouse can lose his or her job, thus jeopardizing the entire family system.

ONLINE PORNOGRAPHY, SEXUAL INDULGENCE AND AFFAIRS: A BETRAYAL OF TRUST

Perhaps the most devastating online addiction a spouse can deal with involves sexual content and behaviors. Whenever a person looks outside the marriage to indulge sexual fantasies or to find sexual satisfaction, the spouse of that person experiences a range of emotions from anger to zeal. The existence and intensity of these emotions can catch one unaware and throw stability out the window. For instance, Maria, a mother of four teenagers and Sam's wife for twenty years, could not believe the emotions stirred up by her husband's addiction to sex chat rooms. At first she was almost more distraught by the knowledge that she could feel rage and hatred than she was by her husband's behavior. In her therapy session, she kept repeating, "I don't believe I can feel this way. I've never hated anybody. I've never wanted to destroy anything as much as I've wanted to whack his computer to pieces. I didn't know I could be this angry, this enraged." Before Maria could even begin to deal with the issues around her husband's addiction, she had to acknowledge her own feelings and begin the difficult work of integrating them into her sense of self.

On the other hand, Sam kept stating that he didn't understand what Maria's problem was. He sloughed his behavior off as "harmless entertainment that doesn't hurt anybody." Sam's attitude mirrors that of many people involved in online affairs or using sexually explicit Web sites. To them their spouse is overreacting because there has been no physical violation of the marriage vows. Because they limit the definition of infidelity to physical, sexual contact—and some even restrict its meaning to actual intercourse—they do not perceive their actions as harmful or even distressing.

Nothing could be further from the truth. Marriage is not a license for sex. In the Pastoral Constitution on the Church in the Modern World, the Second Vatican Council affirmed that married couples "help and serve each other by their marriage partnership; they become conscious of their unity and experience it more deeply from day to day."[10] This type of intimacy is mutually exclusive; it involves the whole person and goes beyond the physical. It also encompasses a person's emotional, psychological and spiritual nurturance and well-being.

While it is true that no one person can meet all of another's needs—and thus the legitimacy of married partners having various circles of friends—sexual intimacy in all its forms is reserved for one's spouse. When a person's online behavior detracts from the time and quality of sharing with one's part-ner, the marriage itself is seriously affected. If a spouse is feel-ing hurt by online behavior and considers it a problem in the marriage, it is a problem.

Maria's insights sum up the feelings of many. "He thinks everything is OK because he has no actual contact with the peo-ple in the chat room. But he's telling them how he feels, sharing his dreams with them and indulging in sexual fantasies. And the more time he spends sharing with his online friends, the less time he spends with the family and with me. What really hurts is that he's always been kind of shy about discussing anything to do with sex, and now he seems to have no reservations at all when it comes to the chat room. I've also noticed that he's become even more withdrawn with me—it seems like he can barely stand to touch me anymore. I tried a few times to initiate some intimate contact; the last time he got up out of bed and turned on the com-puter. I was devastated and cried for most of the night."

There are probably as many reasons for online infidelity as there are people engaging in them. However, some common threads have emerged and to no one's surprise, they are similar to the reasons given for real-life affairs.

RISK FACTORS IN A MARRIAGE

Maintaining a healthy marriage takes time, effort and real com-mitment from both parties. Too often couples allow small things to mushroom into huge issues because they did not have the foresight or courage to resolve the problem when it first appeared. Sometimes couples learn after being married that there are significant differences in the way they approach life and these differences, if not understood and negotiated, can easily become insurmountable obstacles or the excuse for online or actual infidelity. In this section we look at some of these common pitfalls.

Poor communication skills or an unwillingness to communicate sabotage many marriages. This problem knows no social, economic or educational boundaries. Even couples who are normally articulate and communicative often have no clue how to discuss divisive or sensitive matters that may require consensus or compromise. Sometimes a partner's raw emotions, such as feeling threatened, insecure, angry, guilty or overwhelmed, prevent that partner from introducing a topic that is uncomfortable. In the worst-case scenario one partner has been dissatisfied with the relationship for a long period of time and has been unilaterally processing his options without including the other. When a decision is reached, the partner presents it as a "done deal" that hits the spouse broadside and leaves her reeling.

Different priorities and the failure to understand or even try to understand the other's point of view can cause mayhem in a relationship. When a couple does not agree on essential aspects of their lives, the temptation is strong to do what one thinks is right and ignore the other. If one partner is totally focused on work, a career and financial security and the other is absorbed and consumed by the children's needs, the fundamental relationship will erode. Partners will find themselves alone and lonely too much of the time and the length of time between meaningful encounters will grow increasingly longer. This failure to nurture the basic marriage relationship opens the door to an online addiction, especially if one of the partners is prone to addictive behavior of any kind.

A divergence of dreams and expectations can also harm a marriage. As humans we cannot escape the fact that growth demands change on many levels and life is a process. Even in the best of circumstances when a mature couple has adequately discussed key aspects of their future together, a change in dreams and expectations is inevitable. Frequently, one spouse has the sense that he or she is growing—stretching old boundaries and embracing new ideas while the partner remains the same. The complaint that is heard over and over again in therapists' offices is, "He or she is not the person I married. I just want us to go back to the way we were before." But there is no going back for the one who is moving forward.

Sam and Maria's story illustrates this point. Sam blamed Maria for his Internet addiction because "she was into stuff I couldn't care less about. She used to be willing to sit and watch sports with me; it was great because we spent a lot of time together. Now she wants us to *do* things together on weekends. I'm tired and I need to relax. Running all over the place in my free time is not my idea of relaxing. So she started doing things by herself or with her friends on the weekends. If she'd been home, I wouldn't have gotten bored and I certainly wouldn't have turned to the Net and sex chat rooms."

Needless to say, Maria had a different perspective on the problem. "I realized one day that I was tired of watching sports week in and week out. When I suggested that we spend one weekend riding in the country, he threw a fit. I decided that I had a right to relax too, and so I started going to estate sales and antique stores with some friends or by myself. When I came home early one afternoon, I caught him on the computer in a sex chat room. He said it was all my fault, and from then on he didn't bother to hide the amount of time he spent online or try to cover up what he was doing."

Transitional times, whether expected or not, can be challenging to both husband and wife and to their relationship. Frequently, these transitions are laden with danger and opportunity; in fact, the Chinese symbol for crisis is a combination of those two words. Some of the more common transitional times include job or career changes; the completion of major goals; the birth, serious illness, injury or death of a child; caregiving responsibility for aging parents; empty-nest syndrome; health issues pertaining to self or spouse. With the arrival of these events, each spouse must develop coping skills in order to maintain his or her own health. Stress and tension are usually very high during these periods, and there is a legitimate need to reduce stress. One way of doing this is to zone out at the computer. But what constitutes appropriate stress release and what signals the onset of addictive behavior?

Appropriate stress release comes with boundaries. The baby cries and is picked up or checked on; the doorbell or phone rings and is answered; dinner is made pretty much on time; daily tasks are completed in a reasonable fashion; obligations are met; the person feels somewhat relaxed after the computer session. When the behavior is signaling an addiction, the boundaries go out the window and ending the computer session produces anxiety and the craving to return to the online world.

ADDRESSING ONLINE ADDICTION IN A MARRIAGE
When one spouse is struggling with Internet addiction, the other person usually goes through an emotional roller coaster. Feelings of self-doubt, worthlessness, depression and poor self-esteem can overwhelm or even emotionally paralyze the

nonaddicted person. The spouse addicted to the Net has his or her own issues to contend with. And then there is the marriage relationship itself that is being damaged. For all these reasons, professional help is the best recourse. Given the complexity of the issues, a therapist might suggest individual, couples and addiction counseling—either concurrently, in a rotation or progressively. If either spouse refuses to seek help, the other spouse should follow through on his or her own.

DISCERNMENT

In today's world, with ever-escalating divorce rates and a casual attitude toward the sanctity and lifelong commitment of Christian marriage, society would endorse and even encourage a rapid exit from a marital relationship in which one spouse is addicted to the Internet, particularly if the addiction involves sexually explicit content. However, the faith-filled person recognizes that such a decision cannot be made hastily or without proper deliberation. What follows is a discernment process that honors the role of faith and spirituality in one's daily life as well as the need for careful, thorough assessment and evaluation.

Pray for the guidance of the Holy Spirit: Before undertaking any major project or decision, the Christian invites the Spirit of God into the process, particularly asking for openness to what is discerned and freedom from any obstacle that would prevent one from hearing and responding to God's voice.

Gather the facts: A person cannot make an informed and just decision if one does not have accurate information. What do you know to be true of your spouse's addiction? How much time does your spouse really spend online? Do you know what type of online activity in which he or she engages? Is it illegal? For example, does it involve sexual content with children or tax evasion from gambling or gaming payoffs? What effects has the addiction had on you? On the family? If you decide to leave, can you support yourself and your children? Where would you live? Has your spouse made any effort at recovery? These are just some of the typical issues that a person needs to consider, but each situation will also have unique aspects that need to be factored into the overall decision.

Identify gospel values: Prayerfully reflect on the Gospels, the teachings of Jesus and the other New Testament writings and name the values that your decision encompasses. Do not be surprised if you discover some apparent contradictions—at this point, the important thing is to recognize that the Gospel is relevant to your situation. Two gospel values that illustrate this point are Jesus' and Paul's teachings about the meaning and sacredness of marriage and the early church practice of excluding a member from the community for grave reasons, always with the hope that the isolation would lead the person to repent and return. Both of these gospel values have something significant to say to the believer who is torn between staying in a marriage and leaving it, either temporarily or permanently.

Reflect on church teaching: One does not have to be a theologian to complete this step of the discernment process but an awareness of what the church teaches adds another dimension to the process. Often it is helpful to seek some outside guidance when working this step. Consider talking with a priest, a high school or college theology teacher, or call the person in charge of the Family Life Office for your diocese.

When it comes to marriage, some would say church teaching was obvious. Yes, there is a consistent teaching on the permanence of a sacramental marriage. But there is also a consistent teaching on a parent's responsibility to protect and nurture children, to bring them up in an environment that constitutes a domestic church. There is also clear and unequivocal teaching about the primacy of conscience, which in the final analysis, cannot be violated.

Seek input from others: Inviting a qualified person to companion you through the discernment process makes room for the Holy Spirit to affirm, confirm, expand or challenge your thinking. A qualified person may be a confessor, a spiritual director, a pastoral minister, a professional counselor or even a faith-filled friend with the gift of wisdom. We seek a companion on this journey because Jesus tells us, "For where two or three are gathered in my name, I am there among them" (Matthew 18:20).

Make the decision: As a person proceeds through this process, a direction emerges that seems the best possible choice. Even though there is always the possibility of making a mistake (our human limitations guarantee that option!), the person who has conscientiously and prayerfully discerned a decision needs to act on it. Years ago at some retreat or workshop, the presenter handed out a simple exercise that has proven invaluable over the years. In its simplicity, it brings together head and heart and makes clear the direction one needs to take. Patrice has successfully used it herself, with retreatants, spiritual directees and clients, and shares it here.

A DISCERNMENT EXERCISE

The best that can happen if I ...	The worst that can happen if I...
The best that can happen if I do not...	The worst that can happen if I do not...

DIRECTIONS FOR USING THE DISCERNMENT EXERCISE:

1. Find a quiet space and time to begin this exercise and place it in the context of prayer, asking the Holy Spirit to guide you.

2. State the issue in a simple phrase and do not use negatives in your statement. For example, write "if I leave," rather than "if I do not stay."

3. Write the same phrase in each of the four boxes.

4. Begin jotting down words and phrases that come to mind for any of the four sections. Do not be surprised if you find yourself writing many statements for just one or two of the quadrants and feeling stuck about what to put in the others.

5. Stop writing when you feel that you have done as much as you can for the moment.

6. Keep the chart handy; over the next week you will be amazed at the odd moments when you think of something to put in one of the boxes. Add to it as inspiration strikes.

7. Within seven to ten days of beginning the chart, find quiet space and time. Again ask the Spirit to guide your reflection. Then slowly read each section.

Highlight or circle the phrases that resonate within you. Reread these statements. In which quadrant are they? What does this information tell you? Also be aware that you may have multiple items highlighted in one section and only one in another, but the impact of the one is so strong that its very placement tells you all you need to know.

Test your decision: The final step in any discernment process is to take the acid test provided in Galatians 5:22–23: "...the fruit of the Spirit is love, joy, peace, patience, kindness, generosity, faithfulness, gentleness, and self-control." If, despite the difficulties of following through with the discerned decision, you can stand before God and yourself and know within you these gifts, especially "the peace of God, which surpasses all understanding" (Philippians 4:7). You can confidently surrender your decision to the mercy of God.

· CHAPTER 6 ·

Parents, Children and Online Dangers

Blessed are the pure in heart, for they will see God.

—Matthew 5:8

The Internet has emerged so rapidly and dramatically as a popular educational tool for children that most parents don't know what to make of it all. Unable to keep up with all the new and conflicting information about what the Net really is, how it works and what it can and can't do for their kids, parents tend to feel overwhelmed by all the technology. Moreover, many are still grappling to understand the rudiments of computer literacy while their children seem to be masters of all things digital, remote controlled and computerized. Worst of all, as parents hear stories about online pornography and cyber predators, they worry about what their children are really doing online and how best to protect them.

"Everyone says that kids need to learn computer technology," these parents tell themselves. "They use computers in the schools all the time now, so I should get Jenny her own personal computer for her bedroom so she can practice at home. On top of that, she needs to actually use a computer and the Net to complete some of her homework and long-term assignments. She's got to keep up with the other kids." And the fact of the matter is that children *do* need to learn how to use computers and be comfortable with the ever-changing and emerging forms that the technology develops. In their world, educational and career opportunities will be strongly linked to the ability to navigate through layers of technology.

But if you, as a parent, don't even know how to turn on a computer, have never received or sent an e-mail message, or you are in the dark about the workings of the Internet, then you don't know how your child is being introduced to and interacting with it. "But," you figure, "whatever she's up to surely has to be better than wasting all her time watching television, because the Internet is *educational*." So you don't get involved, don't ask many questions, don't monitor online time and activities. You shrug your shoulders and say to yourself: "My kid knows more about this stuff than I do."

The Hidden Dangers

The Internet has fast become a tool that children at younger and younger ages are utilizing. However, many parents fail to understand the hidden dangers of the Internet when they leave children unsupervised at the computer. These dangers are so rampant and perilous that the television industry has taken notice: Numerous local, national and cable networks have aired news segments, talk shows or documentaries about children and the Internet. NBC, in particular, has highlighted the problem by airing a series called "To Catch a Predator" during its *Dateline* news program. During the program, undercover police officers pose as underage children and arrange meetings with potential child predators who are anticipating sex. Once the predators arrive, they are greeted by armed police officers and are arrested. The purpose of the program is not only to "catch a predator" but also to make people aware of the very real dangers of online chat rooms and how the dangers are exacerbated when children have unrestricted and unsupervised access to the Net.

In this section we name and explain some of the more common dangers that lurk on the other side of our children's keyboards.

CYBER PEDOPHILES

Cyber pedophiles are those who prey upon children online. They pretend to be children themselves as they earn the child's trust and gradually seduce them into sexual and indecent acts or make arrangements to actually meet the child. Often this happens as the unsuspecting parent sits in the next room. Parents need to educate children on the dos and don'ts of talking with strangers on the Internet.

Patrice worked with a teenager who had become e-pals with an inmate in a state maximum-security prison; the man had told her client that he had been in prison for ten years for a misdemeanor. The young woman, who had poor social skills, was enchanted by the offer of friendship, and the romantic, sexual tone of the prisoner's messages. However, when he began to send messages that he was being released and wanted to come visit so he could "take her away and teach her to be a woman," the teen became frightened and disclosed the relationship. Patrice worked with the girl and her parents. The parents decided to contact the warden, and within hours, the Web site was shut down.

Access to Pornography

Access to pornography is easy and often inadvertent. Adult entertainment is the largest industry on the Internet, making it easy for children to bump into hardcore and graphic pornography. A child innocently researching a paper for school can accidentally come across online pornography due to its sheer abundance. One reason for this is that many pornographic sites have names that are similar to Web addresses associated with legitimate and popular sites for children; the only difference is the domain closing, i.e., ".com" instead of ".gov." A distressed parent shared with Patrice that her child's elementary class, which was supposed to be viewing pictures of the nation's capital, saw a few seconds of explicit sexual content when the teacher mistakenly brought up a pornographic site by using the wrong domain closing on the Web address for a historical building.

Protecting children from exposure to online pornography does not have an easy solution. Software that monitors or filters out unwanted sites is only a limited and partial solution because new adult sites incorporate technology designed to get around the restrictions. Many parents are unaware of the extent of online porn and do nothing to prepare their children for when they come across it. Online pornographic sites are a potential problem even for parents who carefully watch their children's computer activity at home because parents cannot always protect their children at school, in the library or at a friend's home.

Inappropriate Content

Inappropriate content flourishes on the Web. Monitoring software directed at screening out pornography does little to stop children and adolescents from reading other kinds of inappropriate content. The uncensored environment of the Internet makes this possible. Government and law enforcement agencies have focused on the sexually explicit content available online, but little has been discussed about the abundance of violent material, hate sites, torture and other things that parents would rather not be so accessible to children, such as how to make a bomb. All of this—and more—is just a few clicks away from any child using the Net. Parents, legislators, school personnel and all responsible adults need to become much more proactive about the types of material children can be exposed to when online.

Violent Games

Violent games abound online and children who play them have helped to answer questions about the influence of media violence on children today. In the wake of several tragic school shootings over the past few years, our culture has begun to realize what research has already shown: Children who frequently play violent computer games such as *Doom* display more aggressive behavior. This connection between playing violent games and the tendency to be violent is real. In fact, the United States military uses virtual war games to desensitize soldiers preparing to be deployed to war zones. While not 100 percent effective, this technique has proven to be a powerful military tool.

Parents need to carefully monitor the type of computer and interactive online games their children are engaged in and provide constructive alternatives. Research on the long-term effects of repeated exposure to violent content and aggressive online gaming is sparse, but many psychologists find a strong correlation between violent content and aggressive behavior. With this in mind, parents need to consider and better regulate the types of games their children play online as well as the types of friends children make within these virtual environments. Without guidelines and adequate supervision, children risk falling into unhealthy and potentially dangerous patterns of behavior.

INTERNET ADDICTION IN CHILDREN

Internet addiction among children is a growing problem. The prevalence and popularity of computers in homes and schools contributes to this problem. Children may be more susceptible to Internet addiction because they live in an age when using the Internet is acceptable and encouraged. Many parents rely on the computer to occupy their children's time, mistakenly believing that their child is safe because she is at home and within sight. These parents do not consider that online chat rooms, instant messaging, interactive games and even eBay can lead to psychological problems for children if not carefully monitored.

One Mother's Story

"My son was kicked out of school because of his obsession with playing *EverQuest*," explains Sarah, a mother of a fifteen-year-old high school sophomore. "He was addicted, plain and simple. He began spending less and less time going out with his girlfriend and other friends, watching television, sleeping—everything was about the game." His mother explained how her son had sacrificed everything so he could play for hours, ignoring his family, quitting his job and losing himself in a three-dimensional virtual world where thousands of people worldwide adventure in a never-ending fantasy.

In the virtual world of *EverQuest*, players control their characters through treasure-gathering, monster-slaying missions called quests. Success makes the characters stronger as they interact with other players from all over the real world. "It all started so innocently," she explains. "But after his first year in high school, his grades started to plummet. We didn't understand why until we confronted him and discovered he had been playing the game. He told us he would do better, and we believed him, but the next quarter he failed nearly every course. It wasn't until he quit the baseball team that I knew something was seriously wrong. He loved baseball too much and dreamed about playing professionally. Now nothing else mattered to him except this one game."

As a result, her son's life went into a downward spiral. His girlfriend broke up with him; he lost touch with all his real-life friends, and he was expelled from school.

"His father and I became worried and tried to set time limits, but he just got mad. I mean, he spoke angrily and hatefully toward us. It was a side of our son we had never seen. All he wanted was the game. Our family doctor told us it was a phase and to ignore it, but we couldn't. I knew this was more than a phase—it was an obsession—and we were frightened and didn't know where to turn."

Parents around the globe are increasingly concerned about their sons' and daughters' online habits. They know that there is a problem, but counselors unfamiliar with online addiction do not understand how seductive the Internet can be. As her son's grades plummeted and his behavior became more self-destructive, this mother continued to look for help and even contacted two local addiction rehabilitation centers. "They all told me it was a phase and that I should try to limit my son's game playing. They didn't understand that I couldn't. He had lost touch with reality. My son lost interest in everything. He didn't want to eat, sleep or go to school. The game was the only thing that mattered to him. When I finally took away the computer, he yelled, screamed and even pushed me. This isn't my son. He's a loving boy. Now I don't know who he is."

THE EMOTIONAL COSTS

Online access is a vital part of the modern world and an important tool in the education of our children. It is present in schools, homes and even shopping malls. Mastering the use of the Internet is likely to be an important skill for those entering the job markets of the future. In addition, it is a highly entertaining and informative medium. However, these very qualities also make it an enticing escape for many children. They can be anyone in an online chat room or play thrilling and challenging games against other players from all corners of the globe. With the click of a mouse, they can enter a different world where the problems of their real lives are no longer present, and all the things they wish that they could be or experience are possible.

Like addiction to drugs and alcohol, the Internet offers children and adolescents a way to escape painful feelings or troubling situations. They sacrifice needed hours of sleep to spend time online and withdraw from family and friends to escape into a comfortable online world that they have created and shaped.

Certainly, not every child who goes online faces the same level of risk. Some children go online and never engage in any kind of addictive online behavior, while others cling to the Internet as a way of coping with problems in their lives.

Children who lack rewarding or nurturing relationships or who suffer from poor social and coping skills are at greater risk to develop inappropriate or excessive online habits. Because they feel alone, alienated and have problems making new friends, they turn to invisible strangers in online chat rooms looking for the attention and companionship missing in their real lives. They may come from families with significant problems, and they cope with their problems by spending time online. As one girl explains, "Whenever I would hear about people being addicted to the Net, I'd laugh. I never even looked at myself and thought about how much my love for the computer had grown. I have social anxiety disorder that developed after my mom divorced her second husband and we moved. At first I had tons of friends; I was popular; I had a great boyfriend. Then my disorder worsened. I was scared to go to my classes or go out in public. My boyfriend ended up cheating on me and leaving me. I was so depressed that I dropped out of school and even lost my friends. That was devastating. I'm now struggling to get through high school, but my social anxiety is still a problem, and I use the Net to cope."

Trying to find one's own identity and growing up in the age of the Internet can be difficult. It is a particularly tricky issue when children go online at younger and younger ages. Even with a modest amount of Internet use, changes can occur in a child's emotional development. They learn to avoid problems instead of dealing with them head-on, or they cope with painful feelings by using the Internet instead of getting the help they need. Socially, they learn to instant message friends rather than develop face-to-face relationships, which can impact their way of relating to peers. As one principal told us, "The Internet is hurting their ability to work in groups. Our teachers struggle to get them to participate in any kind of team assignments; instead they would all rather stare at the computer. When I observe them talking to one another in the hallway, I see young girls who are socially aggressive or inappropriate, and I can't help but think that the Internet is socializing them in ways that emotionally stunts them and makes it difficult for them to deal with others in the real world."

WHAT CAN PARENTS DO?

The first line of protection for a child is awareness and education. Most parents have no qualms about beginning "stranger danger" education with very young children. As a child grows, the information increases: Parents and teachers discuss the potential danger of accepting rides, food or drink or requests to search for lost children or pets from any stranger. We also give our children clear instructions about where and how to find help if they or a friend find themselves in an uncomfortable situation. Yet we turn our kids loose on the Net—where literally thousands of strangers can have access to them. And too often we fail to teach and emphasize even the most basic survival skills: not giving out any personal data, addresses or phone numbers, school attended, parents' names or places of work, type of car and license plate number, upcoming events they or family members will be attending, or information about their and their families' daily routines. Even the most cursory perusal of Web sites such as MySpace, a social networking site in which users create personalized pages, reveal an astounding amount of personal information—all placed out on the Web where anyone can access it (although pages can be made private). In addition to teaching children about "online stranger danger," parents need to spell out consequences for violating the house rules for using the Internet—and consistently enforce them.

Despite a parent's best efforts, some children will still be lured by the Internet, ignore parental teaching and spend way too much time online. As an Internet addiction develops, children may experience symptoms that include: withdrawal from family, friends and activities; anxiety, depression, or irritability; trembling hands, restlessness and sleep disturbances; obsessive thinking or fantasizing about the Internet. While online they may feel uninhibited and experience an increased sense of intimacy. Relationships in the real world may be neglected as those in the virtual world increase in importance. Academic performance is also likely to suffer. If you suspect that your son or daughter is showing signs of being addicted to the Internet, a carefully planned approach needs to be developed. Some basic communication rules apply. You want to be clear about your goals with your child and wait for a quiet, stress-free time to talk. You need to decide what you want to say, use non-blaming language and listen empathetically to your child's response. But the challenges of communicating with children about Internet addiction—or almost any sensitive issue—require special skills and considerations.

1. ADDRESS THE PROBLEM

In a two-parent household, it is critical that both parents present a united front. As a parent, each of you must take the issue seriously and agree on common goals with your spouse. Discuss the situation together and if necessary, compromise on your desired goals so that when you approach your child, you will be on the same page. If you do not, your child will appeal to the more skeptical parent and create division between you.

In a single-parent household, the parent needs to take some time to think about what needs to be said and to prepare for the likely emotional response from the child. A child who is addicted to the Internet or becoming addicted to it will feel threatened at the very idea of curbing computer time. A single parent needs to be prepared for an emotional outburst laden with accusatory phrases designed to make the parent feel guilty or inadequate. It is important not to respond to the emotion—or worse yet, get sidetracked with a lecture on disrespect. Acknowledge your child's feelings but stay focused on the topic of his Internet use.

2. SHOW YOU CARE
It will help to begin your discussion by reminding your child that you love him and that you care about his happiness and well-being. Children often interpret questions about their behavior as blame and criticism. You need to reassure your child that you are not condemning him. Rather, tell your child you are concerned about some of the changes you have seen in his behavior and refer to those changes in specific terms: fatigue, declining grades, giving up hobbies, social withdrawal.

3. ASSIGN AN INTERNET TIME LOG
Tell your child that you would like to see an accounting of just how much time he spends online each day and which Internet activities he engages in. Remind him that with television you can monitor his viewing habits more easily, but with the Internet you need his help and cooperation to become appropriately involved. Put him on the honor system to keep the log himself for a week or two to build trust between you. If your child balks at this idea or clearly lies in his log, you are likely dealing with his denial of addiction.

4. BECOME MORE COMPUTER-SAVVY
Checking history folders and Internet logs, learning about monitoring software and installing filters all require a degree of

computer savvy. It is important for every parent to learn the terms (both technical and popular) and be comfortable with the computer, at least enough to know what your child is doing online. Take an active interest in the Internet and learn about what type of chat rooms your child visits, what type of games your child plays and where your child likes to hang out in cyberspace.

Another aspect of computer use concerns the abbreviated language that is such a staple of cyber culture. Log onto MySpace.com or Facebook.com or another similar Web site, and do a search for your own child's "space." Try to read some of her postings. If you can't find your own child's space, look at others' postings. Chances are that you will feel as if you were reading some language totally foreign to you. If you suspect that your child is spending too much time online or is engaging in potentially harmful exchanges, consider making and enforcing the rule that all of his or her dialogue be written in plain English. Then set about learning the more commonly used abbreviations and emoticons (symbols for feelings)—and ask your child to help teach you. (In fact, there are Web sites that explain popular chat room language and symbols.)

5. SET REASONABLE RULES
Many parents get angry when they see the signs of Internet addiction in their children and take the computer away as a form of punishment. Others become frightened and force their children to quit cold turkey, believing that is the only way to get rid of the problem. Both approaches invite trouble: (1) Your child will internalize the message that she is bad; (2) She will look at you as the enemy instead of an ally, and she will suffer real withdrawal symptoms of nervousness, anger and irritability. Instead, work with your child to establish clear boundaries for limited

Internet usage. Allow perhaps an hour per night after home-work, with a few extra weekend hours. Stick to your rules and remember that you're not simply trying to control her, but are working to free her of a psychological dependence.

6. MAKE THE COMPUTER VISIBLE

Move your child's personal computer out of his bedroom and into the more visible kitchen, dining or living area. You do not want to stare over his shoulder every minute he is online, but walking by now and then in the course of your normal home activities sends the message that the Internet is not something that can be used on the sly. As you will recall, an insistence on privacy for Internet time usually indicates that the user is doing something he wants to hide. If your child needs privacy to write a paper on the computer, allow him to move it back to the bed-room temporarily.

7. ENCOURAGE OTHER ACTIVITIES

When you cut down your child's Internet time, she will be look-ing for something to do, not only to fill in the hours but to achieve a comparable "high." Help her find alternative endeavors, whether it is something she used to enjoy or something new, like a club at school. Talk to her about what she most enjoys on the Net so you can steer her toward a healthy alternative. If she especially enjoyed taking on many different handles online and acting in the character of those different personalities, encourage her to audition for the school play. And remind her that she still can have the same fun on the Internet—only within limits.

8. SUPPORT, DON'T ENABLE

Parents often fall into an enabling role with an Internet-addicted child. They cover up or make excuses for their children when they miss school or fail to meet deadlines, and in the name of keeping peace, they give into their children's demands when they complain loudly. If your child does rebel against your intervention efforts, let the first storm subside. Acknowledge his feelings—it is not easy for him to feel that you're tugging at his only lifeline—but stick to your goals. Validate any effort he makes to work with you. Remind him that other kids have had problems with the Internet and that they found a new way. Above all, let him know that you support him in making these difficult changes.

9. USE OUTSIDE RESOURCES WHEN NEEDED
If your child is unable to moderate her Internet usage and the initial problems persist, along with new hostility in your relationship with her, it's best to seek outside help. You might visit a local alcohol and drug treatment program to gather more information about addictions. School counselors can also help alert you to your child's behavior at school. Ultimately, family therapy may be your best bet to help guide your child's recovery, address family strife and heal wounds old and new.

The innocence of a child is a gift to be treasured and protected. Today's media and technology make a parent's task in this regard so much more difficult. At very young ages children are exposed to sexual, violent and hateful images, lyrics and situations that their minds and spirits are not ready to absorb or process. They are simply too young to understand and too young not to be influenced by what they see and hear. Worse yet, in an online environment, children can be approached by an online predator or inadvertently be exposed to sexually explicit material, hurting their normal sexual development and increasing their risk of being seduced by an online pedophile.

The psychological effects of early exposure to inappropriate stimuli, particularly that of a sexual or violent nature, are well documented. But there are spiritual consequences as well. Children know when they have been violated, and something within them dies. Outgoing personalities become shy, withdrawn and fearful; sparkling, alive eyes turn dull and listless. The emerging sense of self is quashed and goes into hiding. A pervasive sense of shame and guilt colors every experience, leading to an overwhelming belief that somehow the very self is flawed or shameful or undeserving of good things. Children who have experienced such trauma need continual affirmation and reassurance.

When parents conscientiously try to help their child develop an awareness of God and God's goodness, they may run into a real stumbling block. The parent's words indicate that God is loving, kind and always present—the best possible Father and Mother that anyone can imagine. And the child wonders why God didn't protect him, why God let "the bad things" happen.

These "bad things" do not have to be actual, physical experiences of evil. The images and sounds found on online hate sites and Web pages devoted to violence or sex can trigger haunting, frightening nightmares or fantasies, particularly for the young. A child caught in this kind of imaginary world has few resources for finding his way back to a healthy reality, and unfortunately many are too ashamed to ask for help.

In a family one person's problems ripple outward and affect every other member of the family. When the person who is hurting is a child, the dynamics between husband and wife often change for the worse. At times the marriage itself is threatened. A single parent will often engage in extremely negative thinking about self; this inhibits the parent's ability to reach out and be available to the child. Over time, this constant focus on what the parent perceives as wrong or inadequate in him- or herself can lead to clinical depression for the parent.

One aspect of depression that is not adequately explained in most of the self-help literature is that depression is a process. The effects of clinical depression often become evident in stages:

1. The physical—fatigue, tiredness, lack of energy;
2. The mental—forgetfulness, impairment in short-term memory; inability at times to retrieve words;
3. The psychological—emotional pain or numbness, thinking in negatives, for example, "I'm no good to anyone"; "I can't!"; "I can't do anything right"; "It's useless to try";
4. The social—withdrawal from family, friends and activities; experience of feeling better while with another in a meaningful encounter, but sense of well-being is short-lived;
5. The aesthetic and spiritual—inability to be awed by nature or beauty in any form; blocking of creativity; lack of interest in and attempts to pray, journal, go to church.

Recovery from depression occurs in the same order. As a person moves toward full-blown depression, she holds onto the aesthetic, creative and spiritual. Prayer may even intensify as the person begs God for help. In recovery all other aspects of a person's life may feel normal and still the spiritual may not have returned. Some people of faith may even feel guilty for having become depressed in the first place—they mistakenly believe that if they had trusted God more, this would not have happened to them. This is the moment to trust in God and to believe that prayer will return if one stays open to the possibility.

· CHAPTER 7 ·

Surfing, Not Studying:
Dealing With College Student
Internet Abuse

The LORD brings the counsel of the nations to nothing;
*   he frustrates the plans of the peoples.*
The counsel of the LORD stands for ever,
*   the thoughts of his heart to all generations.*

—Psalm 33:10–11

"Staying up late at night on the Internet is the best time
I have at school," boasts Carol, a sophomore physics major.
"After a while, it was all I wanted to do, all I thought about. It was
all so fascinating. In the chat rooms I met a woman from Ottawa,
Canada, who was a physics major at a university there. I don't see
many women physics majors where I am. And I became close
friends with a guy living in England who was actually an exchange
student from California. We connected over everything in life!"
Carol got so engrossed in her Net world that she ignored her
studies. A former math and science whiz in high school with
serious career ambitions, she allowed her grades to crash before
recognizing that her new obsession was sabotaging her goals.

At least Carol recognized the problem. Most college students, sadly, do not. And as their numbers continue to soar, colleges have become perhaps the major breeding ground of Internet addiction. Over the last decade the Internet has permeated every aspect of a college student's life while being touted as the premiere educational tool. There are online bookstores, online homework, online classes, online research and even online registration. However, teachers, librarians and computer coordinators have begun to question if the Internet may be having a negative impact on students' study habits and academic performance. More recently, research studies have begun to prove what so many had already suspected: College students are relying on an educational tool that too easily becomes the source of addiction. Here are just a few statistics:

- Colleges such as Texas State and the University of Notre Dame offer help and treatment for Internet addiction.

- In Karen Brody's article "Drop Out Rise a Net Result of Computers" she states that Alfred University administrators claim that academic dismissal rates have more than doubled due to increased Internet use.

- Facebook statistics show 6.1 million college students from over 2,000 colleges use this site.

- According to the Journal of College Development, counselors at the University of Texas at Austin began seeing students whose primary problem was an inability to control their Internet use. One study found that of the 531 valid responses, 14 percent of their students met criteria for Internet addiction.

CAMPUS BLUES

While university officials are pleased that computer labs are filled to the brim with students dedicated to scholarly endeavors, the reality may well be that students are participating in the following online activities instead:

- exchanging e-mail with their real-life friends back home or at other colleges or sending e-mail to their new Internet companions in far-off locales;
- scanning newsgroup postings to stay abreast of the latest information about their favorite movies, TV shows, musical groups, hobbies, sports teams, etc.;
- venting frustrations in chat-room dialogue, participating in online romances or trying out different personas;
- participating in MUD games that never end and that reward one for accumulating online time;
- downloading pornographic photos and other forms of cyberporn;
- endless surfing of Web pages on any and all topics that catch their attention.

ONE STUDENT'S STORY

"All I want is my life back," explains Eric, a nineteen-year-old sophomore at the University of Pittsburgh and an online gaming addict. "It all started so innocently. Three years ago I was one of the most popular kids at school. I got invited to all the parties, got lots of girls, had too many friends. Then I became addicted to an online game called *Counter-Strike*. I've been playing for three years. It's very hard for me to sign off. I wake up in the morning, skip the shower, get on the computer, stay on until the wee hours of the morning; go to sleep; repeat. I don't know how to stop. I've tried. It's just too hard. I heard this is a very common problem, but I really want to get my life back, and I'd give anything to make that happen."

Eric discovered *Counter-Strike* when a friend of his told him about the game in a calculus class. He started gaming at night and then progressed to gaming after classes. "It was like my reward for going to school, but then I started to become obsessed."

Eric explained how he thought about playing the game when he was in class and soon couldn't deal with sitting through classes. He started to skip classes altogether and stayed up late into the night, sleeping all day, eating at his computer and gaming all night. It was a recurrent pattern. He couldn't focus on studying, and he gradually withdrew from his friends on campus. His friends who originally played the game began to play less and less because they didn't want to put as much time into it as he did. Eric went from a 3.6 GPA to a 1.7 the following semester. After Christmas break he promised himself that he wouldn't play as much. When the new semester began, he missed the first day of class, and the second, and then the whole first week. "The whole time I kept thinking to myself, 'Oh, it's only the first week...you hardly do anything anyway.' I went out and I got books—but I didn't go to class. After the fourth week of missing classes, I realized I was in big trouble. By then I spent no time with any of my previous friends, nor did I call my family or my girlfriend at all. I wasn't honest about what I was doing with my days as far as my girlfriend was concerned."

Eric's life completely unraveled by the end of his sophomore year when he failed nearly every class, his girlfriend broke up with him, and he lost his academic scholarship. "I had to come clean to my parents. It was completely embarrassing having to explain to them why I failed school," he lamented. "They had no idea. I hid my gaming addiction well. The only person who knew that I had a problem was my roommate—and I know he thinks that I was completely crazy to have let an online game ruin my entire life."

RISK FACTORS

College counselors have argued that students are the most at-risk population to develop an addiction to the Internet. The typical college encourages Internet use on campus, has computer labs, wired dorms and mobile Internet devices making online access possible anytime day or night. As a result of the ever-growing addiction rate, several universities have started Internet addiction support group services to help students who abuse and offer education to their resident life staff regarding how to intervene with Internet-addicted students. With such widespread access to the Internet, what are the risk factors that contribute to student Internet abuse?

1. Free and unlimited Internet access
When freshmen register, they usually get a student ID card, a meal card and most importantly for some, a free personal e-mail account that generally comes with no online service fees to pay, no limits to time logged on, and computer labs open for their convenience around-the-clock. It is an Internet user's dream.

2. Huge blocks of unstructured time
Most college students attend classes for twelve to sixteen hours per week. The rest of the time is their own to do as they please: read, study, work, go to movies or parties, join clubs or explore the new environment outside their campus walls. Many forget all these other activities and concentrate on one thing: the Internet.

3. Newly experienced freedom from parental control
Away from home and their parents' watchful eyes, college students long to exercise their new freedom. They engage in pranks, talk to friends all hours of the night, sleep with their boyfriends and girlfriends and eat and drink things Mom and Dad would not approve of. Today some of them utilize that freedom by hanging out in chat rooms and instant messaging friends at all hours with no parent to complain about their refusal to get off the computer.

4. No monitoring or censoring of what they say or do online
When they move on to the job world, college students may find suspicious bosses peeking over their shoulder or even monitoring their online time and usage. Even e-mail to coworkers can be intercepted or scrutinized by the wrong party. In college no one is watching. Computer lab monitors tend to be student volunteers whose only responsibility is to assist anyone who needs help understanding how to use the Internet, not tell them what they can or cannot do on it.

5. Full encouragement from faculty and administrators
Students understand that their school's administration and faculty want them to make full use of the Internet's vast resources. Abstaining from all online use is seldom an option—especially as more institutions use distance learning and put entire courses and library resources online. In theory this is a good thing, but in reality students may be using the Internet for everything but homework.

6. The desire to escape college stressors
Students often feel the pressures of making top grades, fulfilling parental expectations and, upon graduation, facing fierce com-

petition for good jobs. Ideally, the Internet should help make it easier for them to do their necessary course work as quickly and efficiently as possible. Instead, they turn to their online friends to hide from their uncomfortable feelings of fear, anxiety and depression.

7. Social intimidation and alienation

With as many as thirty thousand students on some campuses, students easily can get lost in the crowd. When they try to reach out, they often run into even tighter cliques than the in-crowds of high school. Maybe they do not dress right, look right or speak right according to their peers, but when they join the faceless community of the Internet, they find that with little effort they can become popular with new "friends" throughout the country and across the globe. They instantly turn to online companions to hide from difficult feelings, ease loneliness and escape the pressures they are facing.

8. A higher legal drinking age

With the drinking age at twenty-one, undergraduate students cannot openly drink alcohol and socialize in bars. The Internet becomes their substitute drug of choice—no ID is required, and there is no closing hour.

REACTIONS FROM THE IVORY TOWER

College administrators are concerned because they have invested all this money in an educational tool that a significant number of students are using for self-destruction. As college counselors across the country see more and more cases of Internet abuse on campus, they also see that these students suffer from the following problems because of their online abuse:

- lack of sleep and excess fatigue;
- declining grades;
- less investment in relationships with boyfriend or girl-friend;
- withdrawal from all campus social activities and events;
- general apathy, edginess, or irritability when off-line (*cybershakes*);
- denial of the seriousness of the problem;
- rationalizing that what they learn on the Net is superior to their classes;
- lying about how much time they spend online and what they do there;
- trying to quit completely when threatened with possible expulsion because of poor grades, then slipping right back into the same addictive patterns.

Despite the evidence that Internet addiction is detrimental to both the college and the student, denial runs deep in the college environment because packed computer labs provide an even more effective cover than drinking in a crowded bar. When you are sitting among rows of Internet users whose obsessions manifest in eight-hour sessions, no one is going to tap you on the shoulder and say, "Hey, I think you're seriously addicted to what you do on the computer, and you need to get some help." Most students laugh off any suggestion that they are becoming psychologically dependent on the feelings they get from playing Internet games, talking in chat rooms, gambling or shopping online, surfing or even day-trading stocks. "Only foolish adults get addicted to stuff they take or things they do," students counter. "Anyway, I'm not as bad as the geeks with the computer majors who never log off and have to know all the software programs. I can cut back or quit fooling around on the Net any time I want."

Serious trouble can set in. They flunk out of their colleges. Their real-life girlfriends or boyfriends break up with them because all they ever want to do is play on the Net. Their parents explode when they find out their huge investment in their children's college educations are being used to support all-night Internet sessions. They tumble into a major depression when their online steady blips off the screen forever. They experience withdrawal when they try to quit their habit—even if their only motivation was to stay in school in order to keep their free Internet access. At this point addicted students at last decide to seek help.

Because the Internet is a necessary part of campus life, universities and colleges have taken steps to prevent and combat student Internet abuse. Some of their actions include:

1. Raised Awareness

College counseling centers have been at the forefront for helping students recognize that Internet abuse and its potential for addiction have real consequences among students. The College Counseling Center at Texas State, the Center for Counseling and Psychological Services at Ohio University and the Villanova University Counseling Center are just a few of the institutions that have published literature on Internet addiction that helps students understand the symptoms, risks and treatment of the disorder.

2. Prevention and Education

Several universities have sponsored educational workshops for students that talk about the impact of Internet addiction on campus. Based upon the Internet use study conducted at the University of Texas at Austin, the campus has sponsored various resident life training and campus lectures that address Internet addiction. Similar to alcohol awareness and prevention programs on campus, these programs are designed to promote early detection of Internet abuse on campus by educating students, administrators and faculty on the warning signs and risk factors of Internet addiction.

3. Support Groups

Having students seek counseling when Internet-triggered problems arise is probably the biggest hurdle at colleges and universities. Students often dismiss the notion that Internet addiction exists, and while they may think there is a problem when their friends spend too much time online, they don't encourage them to seek help in the same way they would if their friends had an obvious drinking or drug problem. Colleges such as the University of Maryland at College Park have started support groups for Internet addicts to help them recognize that this kind of addiction is a serious matter. The support group also helps students realize that they are not the only ones who have this problem; the very existence of the group makes a statement that help is available.

WHAT YOU CAN DO

If you are one of the many college students experiencing an addiction to the Internet, or at least feel the gravitational pull of cyberspace, try to evaluate just how much the Internet has impacted your life. Here are a few tips and strategies that can help you manage and control your online use:

1. Assess your online time.

Keep a log of the time you spend on each online activity, including chat rooms, interactive games, e-mail, newsgroups, and other Internet usage. How much is too much time online? What types of things do you do on the Internet? Do you chat with friends? Do you prefer to play online games? Do you like to look up information? What days of the week do you typically log online? What time of day do you usually begin? How long do you stay on during a typical session? Where do you usually use the computer? Keeping a careful log will help you become more aware of how you use the Internet and how much time you actually spend online.

2. Recognize what you are missing.

Write down every activity or practice that you have neglected or cut back on since your Internet habit emerged (e.g., spending time with your partner, studying, going to class, hanging out with friends, playing sports or working out at the gym). This is one way to begin to work through the denial that helps you remain convinced that "everything is fine" and "nothing has changed." However, quitting cold turkey usually does not work and may even be impossible for students whose classes or work require computer and Internet use.

3. Enter the social world that the campus offers.

Find a club or organization that matches your interests. Direct your interests: If you like to compose e-mail messages, consider writing a column for your college newspaper or create a writers' circle or poets' society. Talk to classmates after class. Attend school events. Other support avenues include going to your school's counseling and career services centers or in-person support groups.

4. Cultivate a new interest.
Think of a hobby or activity that you have always wanted to try and commit to doing it in place of some of the hours currently spent on the Net. The more fun things you have in your daily schedule, the less you will miss the constant Internet buzz and be tempted to give in to the craving to go back to it.

5. Find external stoppers.
Use the concrete things you need to do and places you need to go as prompts to remind you when to log off the Internet and schedule your time online just before them. If this is not effective because you ignore them, use a real alarm clock to be set when you need to end the session. Keep it a few steps from the computer so you have to get up to shut it off.

6. Incorporate planned Internet time into your weekly schedule.
Internet addiction does not require that a person go "cold turkey" and quit all usage. Scale down your hours intentionally by scheduling specific starting and stopping times. Set a reasonable goal, perhaps cutting your online time by 20 to 25 percent. You may need to stay at the initial reduced time level for two or three weeks before further reducing your online time, and subsequent reductions may need to be at the 10 to 20 percent level. The important thing is to establish a pattern of reducing excessive time spent on the Net. Instead of "one day at a time," practice "one time a day."

Twentieth-century German psychologist Erik Erikson developed a theory of human development that looks at life as a progression of psychological tasks to be accomplished. These same tasks can be looked at from a spiritual perspective. Many college students are at a point in life in which they are working out identity and intimacy issues. In Stage V, adolescents strive to attain a personal identity, a knowing of who they are as person. If they do not succeed, they will experience role confusion and be unsure of their place in the world or how they fit in. In Stage VI, young adults desire and seek intimacy. If they cannot develop the capacity to be intimate with another during this time, they face a future, at least an immediate future, marked by isolation.[11]

Internet addiction—and the problems that it presents—interferes with this pattern of human growth. A person's own unique identity cannot be nurtured or strengthened if she is spending hours online using a made-up persona that is far from reality. The "polishing" effect of being in face-to-face interactions with real people in real situations is also missing: One does not have the opportunity to test one's emerging identity in a social context, to discover gifts and to begin to understand and tame the rough edges.

The student who is spending untold hours online is not available for intimacy. Intimacy, in the context of which Erikson speaks, embraces far more than sexual activity. Sexual intercourse is one very important aspect of intimacy—but not necessary for it to exist. Likewise, every sexual encounter is not an experience of intimacy. An intimate relationship places a person in a covenant with another: I am free to reveal to you who I am, and you agree to love and accept me and vice-versa. If my behaviors need to be confronted, you will love me enough to do that. To achieve this level of trust requires a personal investment of time. The student who is spending more time online than in class does not have the time to nurture an intimate relationship of any kind.

God calls us to know who we are and to be available for an intimate relationship with God. God calls not only humans, but also the entire universe, to manifest biodiversity. From a Franciscan and ecological perspective, it is the uniqueness of each of many parts that most clearly witnesses to the wholeness and mystery that is God. Becoming who we are meant to be is an act of faith and praise and thanksgiving.

Ironically, it is exactly at this point of human development that young people are testing the validity of the values that they have been taught. Many give up the practices associated with their religious upbringing; most question their faith and the teachings of their church. Yet the hunger for religious and spiritual experience may be intact.

PRAYER CONNECTIONS

If you are a college student struggling with Internet addiction and recognize that your addiction takes up much of your time but leaves you unfulfilled on the deepest levels, we would suggest two steps that you can take.

First, make a commitment to read and reflect on the words of Psalm 139 every day. Spend at least ten minutes reading all or part of the Psalm and thinking about what it is saying to you—and what it actually means for your life. The Psalm is printed below, omitting verses 19 through 22.

O LORD, you have searched me and known me.
You know when I sit down and when I rise up;
    you discern my thoughts from far away.
You search out my path and my lying down,
    and are acquainted with all my ways.
Even before a word is on my tongue,
    O LORD, you know it completely.

You hem me in, behind and before,
    and lay your hand upon me;
Such knowledge is too wonderful for me;
    it is so high that I cannot attain it.

Where can I go from your spirit?
    Or where can I flee from your presence?
If I ascend to the heaven, you are there;
    if I make my bed in Sheol, you are there.
If I take the wings of the morning
    and settle at the farthest limits of the sea,
even there your hand shall lead me,
    and your right hand shall hold me fast.
If I say, "Surely the darkness shall cover me,
    and the light around me become night,"
even the darkness is not dark to you;
    the night is as bright as the day,
    for darkness is as light to you.

For it was you who formed my inward parts;
    you knit me together in my mother's womb.
I praise you, for I am fearfully and wonderfully made.
    Wonderful are your works;
that I know very well.
    My frame was not hidden from you,
when I was being made in secret,
    intricately woven in the depths of the earth.
Your eyes beheld my unformed substance.
In your book were written

all the days that were formed for me,
  when none of them as yet existed.
How weighty to me are your thoughts, O God!
  How vast is the sum of them!
I try to count them—they are more than the sand;
  I come to the end—I am still with you.
  . . .
Search me, O God, and know my heart;
  test me and know my thoughts.
See if there is any wicked way in me,
  and lead me in the way everlasting.

Second, wrest yourself away from the computer and volunteer to participate in one community action or service project. Some colleges and universities are making community service a requirement for graduation—if yours does not, drop in at the ministry center and ask about opportunities for helping others. Spending a week helping victims of a natural disaster, building homes with Habitat for Humanity, helping sick or disabled children, serving lunch once a week at a local soup kitchen or doing any kind of hands-on work with and for those who are truly poor and in need—has the power to change one's perspective and to satisfy the need for meaning and purpose in life; it also provides a very valuable alternative for how you choose to spend your time.

CHAPTER 8

Finding Your Vocation and Hearing Your Calling

*[A]nd what does the L*ORD *require of you*
but to do justice, and to love kindness,
and to walk humbly with your God?

—Micah 6:8

Studies show that 70 percent of adult Web sites are hit between the hours of 9:00 AM and 5:00 PM and almost one in five people visit Internet sex sites while at work. Major companies such as Dow Chemical, Xerox and Merck have all fired workers because of Internet abuse. And there is no work or worker immune. From those in the highest positions of status, responsibility and wealth to those in the lowest—workers in all spheres are finding their attraction to the Internet too powerful to resist, creating problems such as poor work performance and job loss. In reality about 25 percent of workers engage in daily Internet abuse of various kinds, costing companies 5.3 billion dollars in lost productivity. As a result, more and more firms are terminating employees for Internet misuse, and addicted workers struggle to understand why they risk their relationships and jobs just to surf the Net.

Any misuse of time in the workplace creates problems for managers, but Internet abuse is particularly difficult. Because corporations rely upon computers to run almost every facet of their business, employee access to the latest, fastest, best-wired computers is a vital component of success. The dilemma is that the very computer that fosters profit is the same computer that makes Internet abuse simple and easy. Consequently, Internet abuse has reached near epidemic proportions in the business world, and companies have become increasingly concerned about its effects and costs. In the foreseeable future businesses will be driven to enforce even tighter controls on employee computer use and impose stricter consequences on those who use their workplace computers inappropriately. As these new statistics and stories show, the Internet not only hinders a person's work performance but also turns people away from their vocational calling and values.

AN ALARMING CONCERN

Internet abuse is not limited to those who work in public offices or corporations. Those who work from home or a private office are even more vulnerable to yielding to their compulsion for the Internet. Statistics do not yet exist about the number of home or small businesses that wash out or go bankrupt because the owner or some employee spends too much work time online.

Most disturbingly, recent reports have documented that numerous clergy and priests have been caught in a web of Internet pornography. A priest working alone in a closed office does not arouse suspicion. People understand that much of a priest's work involves confidential interactions, and the closed door represents a safeguard for privacy. Father Steven Rossetti, director of Saint Luke Institute, a rehabilitation center for clergy and religious, has written an article for *Tidings*, an online publication of the Archdiocese of Los Angeles, stating that priests are part of the forty million United States adults who regularly visit Internet pornography sites. Sadly, Internet pornography is one of the fastest growing reasons for referring priests and male religious to residential treatment programs.

"Internet pornography can entice a vulnerable person, quickly escalating into an addiction," explains Father Rossetti, "The Internet encourages escapism in some users and may lead to a kind of dissociative state. Developing an Internet fantasy life may be used to substitute for one's real life, particularly if one's real life is perceived as unsatisfying."[13]

LOSING YOUR WAY

Jesus focused all of his energy on fulfilling his mission and resisted everything that distracted from it. Called to carry out our own unique missions, we often stumble, become confused and lose our way.

Amanda works as a case manager for a community mental health clinic. She has spent eleven years helping adults who suffer from developmental disabilities find housing, vocational benefits and community outreach services to improve their daily lives. She has loved her work and believed it to be a special calling because working with disabled adults has enriched her personal and spiritual life.

Last year Amanda discovered Internet chat rooms. "At first it was fascinating to meet so many different people; then it grew to be an uncontrollable obsession," she explains.

At forty-five she was divorced, lived alone and had a limited social and dating life. Her work was her identity: Her job gave her purpose, and she found satisfaction in helping and serving others. Once she got involved with chatting, her life changed. When she came home at night, there were people with whom she could share her most private thoughts and feelings. She had always kept her loneliness hidden from family and friends, and the Internet seemed like a godsend. It provided a seemingly safe place where she could interact with others without leaving her one-bedroom apartment.

"It was consuming me," she said. "I felt distracted at work; I couldn't wait to leave to go home to chat. Normally I was the first one in the office; now I come in late almost every day. A few times I've even called in sick just to stay home and chat with my online friends."

Amanda became distraught because she could not break this habit. "I prayed for guidance. I could see that chatting was hurting the way I interacted with my friends and colleagues at work. I became distant. I didn't tell anyone what was happening to me. Worst of all, I was hurting my clients. They depended on me and I was letting them down. One man lost his benefits because I didn't fill out the paperwork for him in time."

Although Amanda was sure she had discovered her life's purpose, she lost her way and drifted off the path of her true calling and vocation. In the attempt to replace what was missing in her personal life, she basked in an infinite sea of cyberspace friends. Excited by the prospect of having people to come home to talk to, she forgot the vocational and spiritual endeavors that had nourished and enriched her life. Her work had provided direction, purpose and personal satisfaction. In her heart she believed that she was doing the will of God by helping the developmentally disabled. Consequently, as her need to go online grew more powerful and consuming, so did her feelings of remorse, guilt and regret.

Like Amanda, workers who start to use the Internet for fun and recreation find that the technology becomes a convenient distraction. They lose their ability to fully concentrate on the tasks at hand and find they are not producing as much because those new games and chat rooms are getting in the way. When workers get hooked on the Internet, they tend to shift back and forth rapidly between legitimate work and interactive Internet play. This makes it more difficult to concentrate on work details, especially when they are spending a lot of time playing interactive games or talking in chat rooms, where little care is given to correct grammar, spelling, punctuation or even logical thought patterns. Anything goes on the Internet, but not so with work details. An unaware manager may wrongly assume that a sudden influx in employee error is being caused by stress at home, when it is really being triggered by bad habits cultivated on the Net.

Employees spending greater time online may ignore all other social activity because of the relationships they are developing over the Internet. Oftentimes once sociable employees shun all coffee break chatter and friendly morning greetings; they consistently turn down invitations for shared lunches or after-hours socializing in favor of their newfound chat-room regulars.

In Amanda's case she eventually found herself even more socially isolated. Before the Internet became an obsession, she had dated and spent time with friends after work. They had started a monthly book club, but Amanda had skipped the last four meetings. She had a standing appointment at the gym with another girlfriend and had stopped going altogether. She had volunteered with another friend at the local animal shelter, and for the last five years had been on its board. She was named board director the year she started chatting on the Internet. Despite this accomplishment, she began to miss board meetings and lied about why she had not attended. Gradually but steadily, she withdrew from all her social and community connections in order to find more time to talk with virtual friends.

She started to chat at work when the company got a new computer system. Instead of returning calls and answering e-mail, she closed the office door and began chatting with her online friends over coffee breaks and lunch hours that stretched into the business day. When coworkers knocked on her door or entered her office unexpectedly, she was frequently startled and temporarily confused, fumbling to make work-related conversation. Amanda, an agreeable and easy to get along with coworker, suddenly balked at requests to work overtime and used the Internet to complain about her boss and work conditions. Eventually, Amanda lost her job when the agency started to monitor the company computers.

FINDING DIRECTION

The Internet provides some measure of relief from discomfort, whether this is relief from anxiety, depression, loneliness, self-consciousness or just a compulsive urge. Addiction clouds judgment, impairs insight and numbs feelings. Abstinence, at least initially, causes psychological and even physical distress because the person has not yet developed alternative ways of dealing with those feelings. When addicted people first stop using the Internet, they are essentially opening themselves to severe distress in the form of increased irritability, moodiness, depression, anxiety or anger. Under these circumstances it is easy to feel as if recovery is impossible.

Many addicts falsely assume that just stopping the addicted

behavior entitles them to say, "I am recovered." But there is much more to full recovery than simply refraining from the Internet. Complete recovery means investigating the underlying issues that led up to the behavior and resolving them in a healthy manner; otherwise, relapse or even new forms of addiction are likely to occur. We have emphasized that Internet addiction most likely stems from other emotional or situational problems such as depression, anxiety, stress, relationship troubles, career difficulties, impulse control problems or sexual abuse. While the Internet is a convenient distraction from these problems, it does very little to actually help someone cope with the underlying issues. Unless attended to, these issues will resurface over and over again in a person's life, sabotaging honest attempts to heal and recover as well as almost every other step in a positive direction.

When Amanda began to understand what drove her to go into chat rooms, she uncovered the loneliness that permeated her life. She saw how she was using online friends as a substitute for the relationships missing in her life. As Amanda dug deeper, she also realized that she viewed herself as obsolete at work. "I think a strong trigger has been turning forty. There is an underlying feeling that I have not accomplished as much as I would have liked with my life, and I have a younger work colleague who is very accomplished, so I kind of feel overwhelmed about competing in this environment. Of course, spending time online just makes things much, much worse. I used to feel good about my job, but now it seems that my younger coworkers are making more money and moving up faster. The more stressed and overwhelmed I became, the more I retreated to the Internet, which only made me fall further behind in my work. I hate myself for all the time I wasted online when I should have been working."

When she was younger, Amanda felt much passion for her work even though her parents, both physicians, wanted her to pursue medicine as a career. In college she fought with them when she told them she wanted to go into social work; they believed social work to be a lesser career choice and pushed medical school to no avail. This was always a sticking point in their relationship. As a result, Amanda felt that she could not share the joys of working with the developmentally disabled with them. She felt isolated from her family during holiday reunions at her parents' home. Online she met Craig, who also felt disenfranchised by his family as a result of a career choice.

"He validated all my negative feelings," Amanda explained. Craig was fifty and an advertising executive. He hated his boss and resented that his younger coworkers were paid more and moving up the corporate ladder faster. Amanda found comfort in knowing that she was not alone in her situation, but Craig's story reinforced negative feelings about her own work. She lost touch with the good things she was accomplishing through her job and detached herself from her colleagues who had also become her friends.

"I lost faith. Maybe I was burned out or just needed to look at my work in a new way, but I couldn't as long as I had Craig to talk to," Amanda said. "He was bitter about his work after twenty-five years at the same company. His negativity rubbed off on me, and our online conversations led to my becoming bitter and resentful. Before Craig I had been very optimistic and spiritual about my life, but all my passion slipped away the longer I spent talking with him."

As we previously discussed, the Internet becomes a way for the addict to self-medicate in order to temporarily run away

from life's problems. Over time, however, this coping mechanism proves to be unproductive and potentially harmful, as the
issues hidden by the addictive behavior culminate in larger and
larger problems.

When unresolved feelings or situations reemerge, they can
erode any sense of accomplishment and undermine abstinence.
Amanda returned to her chat room friends whenever things got
tough at work or when she was feeling lonely because there was
no man in her life. Every time the agency hired another young
recruit, Amanda's underlying feelings of resentment surfaced,
and she turned to her online friends. Each time a same-aged
friend announced an early retirement, feelings of failure overwhelmed her, and she relapsed again.

Confronting a problem head-on is usually the best way to
approach it. If you are dealing with low self-esteem or depression, find healthier ways of dealing with your feelings. If you are
having relationship troubles, enter couples' counseling instead of
turning to the Internet to address those intimacy issues. If you
view porn at work to handle job stress, learn more effective stress
management techniques to help you relax instead of relying on
the Internet. If you suffer from multiple addictions, seek out professional guidance, when appropriate, to recognize the decision
chain that leads to a lapse before it actually occurs. If you are having career troubles, investigate new job options or career paths.
Of course, corrective behavior is easier said than done.

MENDING RELATIONSHIPS
For the addict the Internet is a time-consuming activity, and to
create more time for the computer, addicts neglect sleep, diet,
exercise, hobbies and socializing. The initial loss of the Internet
means an increase in idle time or boredom, which only

increases the temptation to surf, making it vital to find positive ways to fill the void created by not spending time online. For Amanda the Internet had replaced once cherished friends and her calling to serve others. After losing her job, she focused on personal prayer and sought spiritual guidance from a pastoral counselor. As part of her daily recovery, she mended old relationships and asked forgiveness for being so neglectful while she was in the throes of her addiction.

Involving loved ones in the recovery process can be a rich source of nurturing and sponsorship to help maintain abstinence. Once Amanda mustered the courage to speak of her addiction, much to her surprise, her friends were relieved to finally learn the truth and offered comfort, support and encouragement to help her overcome it. Learning that loved ones can accept mistakes takes a tremendous pressure off the addict and provides the support necessary for continued Internet sobriety.

Due to their addiction, Internet addicts often hurt or lose significant real-life relationships. Often these are the very individuals who provided the addict with support, love and acceptance before the Internet came into the addict's life. Their absence makes the addict feel worthless and reinforces past notions about being unlovable. Therefore, it is essential for the addict to amend and reestablish these broken relationships in order to achieve recovery and find the support necessary to fight the addiction. Clearly, making amends won't be easy—the hurt and pain caused by the addictive behavior cuts deep. It also takes great courage to admit wrongdoing and ask forgiveness. However, it is important to acknowledge personal failure and to correct past mistakes. With this type of sincerity, it is possible to rebuild closeness and intimacy—if the other parties are interested or willing to reinvest in the relationship.

A strong word of caution is needed here. Although making amends and rebuilding relationships are major keys to the recovery process, it is not always appropriate; in fact, in can be harmful to another. If the other person has moved on with his life and does not want any contact with the recovering addict, it is incumbent upon the addict to respect the other's wishes in this regard. No matter how much the addict regrets the loss of the relationship, no matter how desperately the addict wants to personally apologize or ask forgiveness, the choice about having the opportunity to do so does not lie with the addicted person. This is one of the consequences and costs of addiction, albeit a difficult one. And no contact means no contact—no letters, notes, flowers, e-mail or even inquiries to third parties if there is any chance the conversation will be carried back to the other. To disregard the other's wishes in this matter is to retraumatize that person.

When a person in recovery has reached the point at which making amends is the next logical step to take, but is being denied the opportunity to do so, the recovering person needs to seek professional help. There are techniques and processes by which a recovering person can internally resolve these loose ends without having contact with the person whom they have hurt.

When an addicted person is ready to begin making amends, it is also the time to foster new social outlets that provide opportunities to make contact with others in meaningful ways, such as getting involved with local church groups, service organizations and community activities. Forming new relation- ships helps maintain abstinence because outside involvement takes you away from the computer and diminishes the social isolation created by the addiction.

RECLAIMING YOUR CALLING

Amanda began the process of reclaiming her ministry by setting new goals: getting proper rest at night and reestablishing her connections with the book club and animal shelter board. After losing her job, she reflected on her vocation and the inner calling to do God's work. Through counseling, she sought guidance and spiritual direction to rebuild her work of serving others. She started to realize that her job had become mechanical and removed from serving others. Her days were filled with paperwork, phones calls or meetings with other caseworkers; she spent little time during the day, if any, directly working with her clients. After eleven years in the same position, she felt burned out and troubled because the aspects of the job that motivated her to be a social worker were no longer present in her actual work.

Feeling stuck in the less emotionally fulfilling tasks associated with her job, she developed resentment toward younger workers who still had their passion and zest for the field. The emptiness she felt in her work was magnified by the loneliness she felt at home each night. It seemed to her that her life was going nowhere and the distance from her parents only increased her feelings of loneliness and despair. She questioned the decision to go into social work and wondered if medicine would have provided a better living. She took a long look at the direction her life was going without satisfying relationships or intimacy and without a job with which to support herself.

As part of her recovery, she started volunteering at her church. She served as a facilitator for their weekly Bible study and served as a lector on Sundays. Her spiritual journey led her to start serving as a youth minister for the overnight church outings. During one overnight she met Lisa, a fifteen-year-old who had an alcoholic father and a mother who suffered from depression. As Amanda counseled Lisa, she realized that she felt as emotionally abandoned by her parents as Lisa did by hers. Amanda remembered the night she had told her parents that she didn't want to go into medicine but had decided on social work. Her parents were furious, and Amanda, an only child, felt that they had abandoned her.

The more Amanda thought about it, the more she realized that her parents had never been supportive of her chosen career. Lacking their approval, she had constantly turned to others in an effort to gain the approval they withheld. She accepted that she had also emotionally pushed people away, creating a tug-of-war within herself. Part of the appeal of the Internet was that she didn't have to make an emotional commitment to chat room friends and she came to understand how transient these relationships really were.

As Amanda helped Lisa through her problems, she also realized how good it felt to do something for teenagers, a very different population from the developmentally disabled. Through prayer she heard God calling her to start a new chapter in her life. In the fall Amanda enrolled in classes to get her master's degree in pastoral counseling and focused on working with children and troubled teens. While her parents still didn't approve, they understood when Amanda told them about her new career. In risking their disapproval, Amanda felt a confidence that she had never truly experienced. She had faith that she was doing the right thing, the work that God had ultimately prepared her to do.

Amanda let go of her Internet friends, realizing how much of an obstacle they had become to forming healthy, real-life relationships. In their place she started making new friends at school and at church. "These were far deeper and richer relationships than any that I had made online," Amanda said. She also met Tom, a retired accountant who volunteered with her at church, and they became engaged later that year. With faith and openness to God's calling, Amanda discovered a new path, one that healed her from past wounds, one that allowed her to step away from the Internet, and one that empowered her to grow spiritually and maintain recovery.

GOD AT WORK

The tradition of Catholic social teaching dates to 1891 when Pope Leo XIII issued the encyclical *Rerum Novarum*, frequently referred to in English as "Concerning New Things." In that groundbreaking document, the pope pointed out that gospel justice demands that workers meet their obligations and give their employees the full benefit of the time for which they are paid.

Although the invention of the computer was years away and almost certainly beyond the imagination of Leo XIII, his words echo down the corridors of time and strike a resounding chord as modern businesses struggle with the problems of Internet addiction.

Abusing computer privileges in the workplace and spending inordinate amounts of time on pursuits unrelated to one's job are not only symptoms of addiction but also a matter of justice. Too often workers addicted to the Internet trivialize their importance and discount the contributions that they make. This attitude invites rationalization about their addictive behaviors at work: "Anyone can do my job; a few hours less of my time won't mean a thing to this company."

Spend some time reflecting on how work is a significant and important part of your life. Perhaps for the first time, look at the work you do in terms of the service you render; ask yourself how God is calling you and using your talents and gifts in the work you do. If you do not think that there is a connection between your work and God's call to you, then you may need to seriously consider a different kind of work or find other outlets to utilize the gifts God has given you. You may also have to come to grips with the reality that you are resisting God's call. If this is true of you, you are in good company: The Bible relates story after story of reluctant hearers of the Word who found excuse upon excuse to avoid responding to God's call for their lives.

PRAYER CONNECTIONS

Find a quiet space and time and complete the following statements in your journal.

• I have been truly happy when…

• If I am honest with myself, I know that God has blessed me with the ability to…

• I give in to my Internet addiction at work because…

• To bring my work, my life and my God-given gifts and talents together, I need to…

Hope and Renewal on the Path to Recovery

[T]he hope laid up for you in heaven...
[T]he hope promised by the gospel...
[T]he hope of glory.

—Colossians 1:5, 23, 27

Internet addiction has been called the silent addiction. Unlike alcoholism, there is no smell of alcohol on the breath to give oneself away and unlike stopping at an adult entertainment store, there is no risk of being seen or recognized. While others may wonder why you spend so much time on the computer, you may be the only one who actually knows that your online behavior signals something deeper and more complex.

Unlike people with other addictions, Internet addicts often realize that they have a problem long before others notice changes in their behavior. As we have discussed, many Internet addicts realize that they are spending less time with family or friends but don't care, or care but can't seem to pull themselves away from the computer.

They see themselves slipping away. They are more interested in chatting with online friends than spending time with their children. They are more interested in visiting online casinos than spending the money on their family. They are more interested in looking at online pornography than having sex with their husbands or wives. They are more interested in shopping on eBay than working toward the next big promotion.

These addicts see their lives and their values changing because of the Internet. They become secretive, hiding what they do online and how long they spend on the computer. They lie to a spouse, telling him or her that they have to work late when they are actually talking to an online lover. They become preoccupied with the Net, telling their children that they can't take them to school or to swim practice. In reality they have the time but have allocated it for more online use. Formerly cherished people, activities and interests start to become less interesting and less important.

Compulsive online users feel ashamed of their behavior. They worry what their spouses would think if their spouses knew what they really did on the computer. The addicted person fears that the spouse or another loved one will take away what has become their escape from pain, problems and stress. They feel like they are leading a double life. Telling anyone what they really do on the computer seems too overwhelming to ever admit. They lose hope that they will ever stop their secret life and carry a sense of shame that keeps them from being open to anyone, including God.

BEING OPEN

Part of the healing process is being open about your addiction. James, at age fifty-two, began using the Internet extensively for work last year. A chemical engineer, he did research online and frequently used e-mail to contact vendors. One night while working late, he discovered online pornography, and within ten months was spending nearly thirty hours a week viewing, downloading and collecting Internet pornography.

James felt overwhelmed by the constant demands at work and felt distant from his wife of twenty-two years. "I guess after the kids left home, it was hard finding things to still talk about."

In time, James realized that the Internet was not meeting his deepest needs, and the effort to keep pretending that all was well became too heavy a burden. James finally admitted to himself that he had an addiction. He acknowledged the damage he had caused to his marriage and his family. He scrutinized his behavior and saw its effects: how little time he spent with his children, how much he had lied to his wife, how his marriage had suffered. He realized how much he had been in denial, rationalizing that he was not doing anything wrong while his wife and he were bearing emotional and spiritual scars. Finally, he admitted to his wife what he had been doing.

His wife was hurt and shocked but with faith they were able to find a new place in their marriage to rebuild the broken trust that had occurred because of the computer.

James started counseling with his wife, who wanted to make their marriage work. She wanted to forgive. He wanted to be forgiven. He was open about his addiction to online pornography. He felt sad that he had let it get that out of hand. He had thought he was in control, but realized that he had been lying to himself, to his wife and ultimately betraying their marriage.

With counseling James realized that when he felt stressed at work he turned to pornography as an outlet. He then understood how he had neglected what once was a sexually fulfilling marriage. James realized that he was still attracted to his wife but his indulgence in online pornography had left him emotionally and sexually drained. The couple established new computer ground rules at home. He took the Internet off his office computer. He made a contract with his wife that he would not look at porn. As they talked, they were able to reestablish trust and intimacy, and they built a new foundation for their marriage, one that included God.

"It opened up a whole new relationship for us," James explained. "We were truthful about many problems in our marriage that had kept us from being truly intimate over the years. We had built something deeper. We prayed together when things got tough, and whenever I felt tempted to look at pornography, I was able to call her. In many ways she became my sponsor through my recovery, and it helped us both to rekindle the type of intimacy we had when we first got married. I'm so thankful to her and so grateful to God for giving me a second chance."

SEEKING PROFESSIONAL HELP

The problem with Internet addiction is that it is still newer than other addictions, so finding qualified help can be difficult, as many therapists and counselors feel unprepared to treat it. With this in mind, when you begin to seek out a counselor, there are a few things you must first consider. Therapists vary greatly in their skill levels and ability to deal with specific issues. Competence in a given field is gained by the degree of training in a specific area, the type of education they have had and the amount of knowledge that they have about the Internet. Specialized and trained professionals in the area of Internet addiction are only slowly emerging. If one isn't available in your area, but you are trying to locate the most qualified healthcare professional, consider these five factors when choosing a therapist.

1. Find a therapist with whom you feel comfortable.
2. Find a therapist who fully comprehends the nature of your problem.
3. Find a therapist with whom you can establish a collaborative relationship.
4. Find a therapist who believes that someone can be addicted to the Internet.
5. Find a therapist who has at least a basic knowledge of the Internet, who understands its scope, potential and problems and who has some familiarity with using it.

In general, entering therapy is a difficult process. It isn't easy to find a therapist familiar with the Internet, online addiction and the impact of online affairs. Over time this will change, but in the meantime, make sure that your therapist is someone willing to listen and learn about the Internet in order to best help you.

THE TWELVE STEPS

Twelve-Step support groups are important in the recovery process. Sharing in the fellowship of those who are also in recovery surrounds the addict with others who have suffered in the same way, helping him to no longer feel alone. Support group participation also helps the addict gain a new sense of pride, improve self-worth, provides encouragement, redefines their core value system and models new ways of interacting.

Though the Twelve Steps were developed by and for alcoholics, they have been been adopted by those who suffer from other compulsive disorders, leading to the formation of other Twelve-Step support groups, for example, Al Anon, Gamblers Anonymous, Overeaters Anonymous, Narcotics Anonymous and Sexual Addicts Anonymous. Using this program, individuals and families who have felt high levels of desperation and pain have been able to turn their lives around.

The Twelve Steps can be applied to recovery from Internet addiction. They are:

1. We admitted we were powerless over the Internet—that our lives had become unmanageable.
2. Came to believe that a Power greater than ourselves could restore us to sanity.
3. Made a decision to turn our will and our lives over to the care of God *as we understood Him*.
4. Made a searching and fearless moral inventory of ourselves.
5. Admitted to God, to ourselves, and to another human being the exact nature of our wrongs.
6. Were entirely ready to have God remove all these defects of character.
7. Humbly asked Him to remove our shortcomings.
8. Made a list of all persons we had harmed, and became willing to make amends to them all.
9. Made direct amends to such people wherever possible, except when to do so would injure them or others.
10. Continued to take personal inventory and when we were wrong promptly admitted it.
11. Sought through prayer and meditation to improve our conscious contact with God, *as we understood Him*, praying only for knowledge of His will for us and the power to carry that out.

12. Having had a spiritual awakening as the result of these steps, we tried to carry this message to others, and to practice these principles in all our affairs.

Accepting that there is a Higher Power is not necessarily about religion, but the Twelve-Step model is a belief system that helps to overcome temptation when hard times occur. Relapse is part of recovery, and having a support group will help you to process those moments of relapse and work through the triggers for your online relapses. Group membership will also help you at the next moment of temptation by providing sponsorship, akin to AA, in order to cope with difficult times during this transition period.

Support groups also help you to address conflicting emotions that underlie the addiction. As you struggle with how to coexist with the Internet and all it offers without indulging, you may also feel angry that you must give up something that makes you feel better about yourself, and you may be resentful of others who are trying to take it away from you. In a group of supporters, you can confront these issues and deal with them in a warm, caring atmosphere.

Often the Internet addict may try to normalize her behavior: "I'm not as bad as so-and-so. She spends more hours online; she lost her job because of it; she lost her marriage, but I'm OK." In reality the addict is not OK. A support group will help you to correct this type of self-destructive thinking that only serves to reinforce the addictive behavior.

Sometimes group participation has the opposite impact, with members becoming competitive with one another about who has the worst battle story. "You did this, but I did that" is the type of mentality shared by some addicts, with each trying to show she is more messed up than the rest. This is a sign of an unhealthy attempt to gain attention from others, and while you may have suffered significantly, you shouldn't characterize your situation as better or worse than others. The gift of support is to help you understand the uniqueness of your situation as well as the common factors you share with others. Most importantly, group membership provides an opportunity for you to develop real life relationships through the support and understanding of other members. This is especially important for Internet addicts who typically suffer from interpersonal difficulties such as introversion, a limited social network and poor social skills. This inability to be at ease with or emotionally connect with others is often what led to the Internet addiction in the first place. In an Internet addict's world, virtual contact is a substitute for the lack of real-life social connections. With the support and help of the group's membership, an Internet addict won't need to rely on online friends for companionship, and these new relationships will empower her to feel less isolated so that the focus stays more clearly on recovery.

CELEBRATING THE SACRAMENT OF RECONCILIATION
For a Catholic, perhaps the deepest prayer connection is to celebrate the sacrament of reconciliation. The grace of this sacrament is a powerful, energizing force that can help one to deal with Internet addiction. In this section we are going to discuss aspects of this sacrament and make suggestions that will help an individual to fully experience the life-giving power that this sacrament holds.

THE SACRAMENT AS PROCESS
From the very first moment that a person begins to consider that he or she would like to celebrate the sacrament (go to confes-

sion), that person has begun the process of reestablishing a right relationship with God, self and others. Generally speaking, a thoughtful preparation for receiving the sacrament enhances one's experience of it. However, sacraments contain a power in themselves that transcends the human, and so one must recognize that a spur-of-the-moment celebration of the sacrament on a Saturday afternoon has the same power and spiritual effects as a well-prepared celebration of the sacrament. What may be different is the penitent's perception and experience of the sacramental grace.

The timing for celebrating this sacrament is also part of the process. One retreatant's story illustrates this point. Matt suffered from a more traditional addiction but had started seeing a counselor and going to AA. As a result, he had been sober for six months, a real accomplishment for him. He was working the Steps and decided that he would like to go to confession because he was beginning to realize how much pain he had caused his family. However, when Patrice asked if he had gone to confession during the active phase of his addiction, his response was, "No, I couldn't. I knew I wasn't ready to stop, so what was the use?"

Matt's answer led to a discussion about grace and the truth that God does not abandon us in our weakness. Certainly, a celebration of the sacrament at a time in life when one is beginning to resolve problems is appropriate and often moving, even exhilarating. However, as Christians we cannot forget that we can come before God in the midst of our chaos and neediness, even when it seems like the very power of hell has broken loose around us. In the midst of this pain, even believing that "I'm not ready or able to change," a celebration of the sacrament of reconciliation can be meaningful—it may even be the agent of change.

PREPARATION FOR CONFESSION

Choosing and Locating a Confessor

Although a confession made to any priest in the world is valid and accesses sacramental grace, a person struggling with Internet addiction should consider the following: Would I be comfortable enough to be radically honest if I make this confession to a priest with whom I am familiar or with whom I interact on a regular basis? Would I feel more comfortable, less ashamed and freer if I confessed to a priest I do not know and who does not know me? Does the priest have at least a functional knowledge of the computer and the Internet? This last is important because there are priests who have no idea what penitents mean when they confess "internet pornography" or an "online affair." For someone struggling to be free of an addiction, this lack of knowledge on the priest's part is not helpful.

If one decides not to confess to the local parish priest, where does one find a confessor? People talk and chances are you have heard comments about a priest from another parish whom everybody loves. You may live near a retreat center or a college or university with a ministry center. There may be priests from religious orders (Franciscans, Dominicans, Jesuits, Augustinians, Benedictines, to name a few) ministering in your area. Local hospitals, even non-Catholic ones, have priests who are on staff or on call, and they usually have had some specialized training in pastoral ministry. If you live in a rural area, your options will be more limited, and you may have to travel. If, despite your best efforts, you do not have access to a priest or you simply cannot confess to the available priest, call your diocesan bishop's office, explain that you need a confessor, and ask for help in getting one.

The choice of a confessor is significant because a person fighting an addiction can expect to want or need to celebrate this sacrament frequently. By selecting a confessor to whom you return for subsequent celebrations of the sacrament, you eliminate the need to repeat your history or provide context for the past every time you go to confession. This can be very freeing. You also eliminate most, if not all, of the anxiety that can be generated prior to confession as you wonder: "What will Father think of me?" or "How is he going to react?" For anyone struggling with an Internet addiction, we strongly recommend that you call the confessor of your choice, identify yourself by at least your first name and last initial, and ask if you can schedule an appointment for confession. This is important because Internet addiction is so often surrounded by anonymity and false persona—and by stating who you are, you break the cycle of hiding behind your screen name. For the same reason, we recommend that you decide to celebrate the sacrament face-to-face with the priest rather than using the anonymity of the confession box. However, if even thinking of a face-to-face encounter jeopardizes your decision to go to confession, give yourself permission to remain anonymous. Today churches have various ways of safeguarding a penitent's anonymity. Some churches retain the traditional confession box, in which a screen separates the priest and penitent; some churches have a screen placed in the reconciliation room; some churches have the chairs in the reconciliation room arranged so that you choose whether to sit facing the priest or not. If you need to use the confessional, inform the priest when you make the appointment so he can be prepared for this option. Otherwise, expect to meet with the priest in his study or in the reconciliation room of the church or chapel.

If you have not been to confession in a long time or don't remember what to say, you can mention this to the priest when you make your appointment and ask if he will guide you through the ritual. Most priests will assure you that this is not a barrier to going to confession and will tell you not to worry—he'll be there to help you.

Many people have also found it helpful when scheduling their appointments for confession to give themselves some quiet time both before and after. This quiet time need not be spent in a church; what is important is to have both a time and a place where you can be alone and undisturbed and free to reflect.

Preparing Your Confession

Most Catholics first went to confession when they were children and were taught a simple formula for confessing sins: We named what we did and tried to say how many times we did it. Just as you have outgrown the clothes you wore to that first celebration of penance, you have most likely outgrown that simple formula. The formula still works but there are other ways to confess sins— ways more compatible with your understanding and maturity.

Our recommendation is that you place your addiction in context. You must still name the sin and be as specific as possible. Instead of saying, "I'm addicted to the Internet," say "I'm addicted to playing games, especially war games, on the Internet," or "I'm addicted to online pornography and spend hours looking at pictures of nude men." Then think about the effects of your addiction on yourself, your family, your friends and your job. Do an honest assessment of how many hours per day or per week that you spend on the computer. As accurately as possible, identify how long this problem has existed and the circumstances in which it started. If you have made any attempts to stop, were you successful at all? For how long? What was driving your inability to stop or what triggered your return to the addiction after experiencing some control? As you stand before God looking at the mess your life has become, do you think you have any control over the addiction? Is it a conscious choice? Was there a point at which you could have stopped but chose not to? Have there been any glimmers of hope? Have you consistently prayed a favorite prayer or Scripture verse? What do you think you need to do to make things better? What step(s) do you need to take to begin the recovery process?

Making Your Confession

Having taken the time to reflect on your addiction, you are now ready to talk about it. In a conversational way, share the details of your reflection with the priest being as forthright, accurate and honest as possible. In this way you bring all the circumstances of your addiction before God, and in so doing, make an act of trust in God's mercy, compassion and forgiveness. If the priest asks any questions, respond as honestly as possible. If you do not know the answer or haven't thought about what was asked, simply say that. At some point you need to either make a formal act of contrition, or in your own words express your sincere sorrow for what you have done as well as your desire not to repeat the problematic behavior. After you have spoken, the priest will assign a penance, pray the prayer of absolution and bring the celebration of the sacrament to a close.

Carrying Out the Assigned Penance

Do not be surprised if the priest asks what you think might be an appropriate penance. If this happens, recall your thoughts about what steps you need to take to begin the recovery process and suggest one of these ideas. The priest may agree with you, adapt your idea, or decide on something entirely different. If you are unclear about what the priest means or do not think you can do what he has asked, it is OK to tell him this. For example, if a priest told you to say the *Memorare* every day for two weeks, and you have no clue what the *Memorare* is and know you won't even remember the word in order to look it up, don't leave until you have asked for an explanation. The priest will then decide whether to change your penance, tell you how to find a copy of this prayer or provide a copy for you.

Use the quiet time you have scheduled for yourself to thank God for the gift of this sacrament, to say any prayers that were assigned as a penance or to plan how to carry out your penance. For example, if your penance is to make and keep an appointment with a professional therapist, make the decision to call your health insurance provider within two or three days to learn the details of the mental health benefits you have in place. This information should help you make a decision about whom to call; then follow through by scheduling the appointment within one week and keeping that first appointment.

FAITH ALONG THE JOURNEY
Continue to look at the possibilities of a new life without having the Internet to control it. You will feel free from the hidden habit of the computer. Achieving lasting recovery is a blessing.

The most challenging aspect of lasting recovery is fighting the temptation to return to the addiction. Relapse is part of recovery. In addiction struggling to fight this temptation is particularly difficult in the early stages of recovery—even with the grace of the sacrament of reconciliation, professional help, Twelve-Step groups and supportive family relationships.

Sometimes it takes sheer will to overcome the urge to use. Understanding your triggers and avoiding situations that lead to relapse are ways to prevent temptation. Sometimes, as with most addictions, the real fight is with inner conflict. Most addicts reach a point in which they want to stay clean and abstain from the addictive behavior, but in moments of stress or loneliness or loss, they are tempted to return to the addiction as a way to escape.

In those moments, know that you are not alone and that God is walking with you. Find a quiet place to reflect and pray. Consider these words of Scripture, "Come to me, all you that are weary and are carrying heavy burdens, and I will give you rest. Take my yoke upon you, and learn from me, for I am gentle and humble in heart, and you will find rest for your souls. For my yoke is easy; and my burden is light" (Matthew 11:28–30).

Recall the times that God has helped you in the past. It may be in small things—things that have happened at work or with your family or friends; it may be during times of extreme turmoil such as working through a painful breakup or the loss of a loved one. God has been there in the past, whether you have recognized this or not. God walked beside you then, and God will continue to companion you now.

In those moments when you are feeling overwhelmed, when the battle seems hard, when those moments of temptation occur, when the journey toward recovery seems long, remember that God is with you. "He gives power to the faint, / and strengthens the powerless" (Isaiah 40:29). God will give you strength. God will give you comfort. God will give you nourishment. Rejoice and do not be afraid. In recovery it is easy to be afraid of the unknown, afraid of life without the Internet, afraid of dealing with all the unresolved problems that existed before you got hooked on the computer. Remember God walks with you. God carries us in suffering. God lifts our spirit. God calms us in moments of trouble and self-doubt. In those moments, when you feel weary and troubled, when you think about returning to your life on the computer, rejoice and do not be afraid. Remember that God is with you.

· NOTES ·

[1] S. Peele with A. Brodsky, *Love and Addiction* (New York: Taplinger, 1975).

[2] Peele.

[3] K. Young, *The emergence of a new clinical disorder*. Paper presented at the 104th annual meeting of the American Psychological Association, August 11, 1996. Toronto, Canada. Published in *CyberPsychology and Behavior*, 1 (3), pp. 237-244, 1998.

[4] Peele.

[5] Thomas Merton, *Thoughts on Solitude* (New York: Farrar, Straus and Giroux, 1958), p. 79.

[6] Regis Armstrong and Ignatius Brady, eds., *Francis and Clare: The Complete Works* (New York: Paulist, 1982), p. 102. Franciscan theology and spirituality is rooted in the belief that God is good and from this derives the goodness that is found in all creation.

[7] *The Confessions of Saint Augustine*, F.J. Sheed, trans. (London: Sheed & Ward, 1944), p. 188.

[8] See http://www.feastofsaints.com/ancientnew.htm. From *The Confessions of Saint Augustine*.

[9] Sigmund Freud, *The Interpretation of Dreams* (New York: MacMillan, 1900), p. xxxiv.

[10] Austin Flannery, O.P., ed., *Vatican Council II: The Conciliar and Post Conciliar Documents*, vol. 1, new rev. ed. (Northport, N.Y.: Costello, 1996), para. 48, p. 950.

[11] http://www.ship.edu/%7Ecgboeree/erikson.html. For more information, choose Anna Freud from the table of contents at the same Web site.

[12] S. Rossetti, "Internet Pornography: Raising the Alarm." See www.the-tidings.com/2006/0303/rossetti.htm. To access, type www.the-tidings.com/2006/0303. Select Viewpoints, then choose "Internet Pornography: Raising the Alarm."

[13] Rossetti.

addiction
  breaking, 9
  in children. *See* children
  church documents on, 4
  defined, 6
  detachment and, 57
  diagnosis, 16
  emotional states and, 11–12
  multiple, 76–78
  negative thoughts and, 12–13
  numbing effect of, 11–12, 24
  patterns in, 15
  process, 6–7
  progressive nature of, 11, 56
    compulsivity, 59–60
    discovery, 52–53
    escalation, 56–57
    experimentation, 55–56
    hopelessness, 60–64
  recovery, 136–137
  risk of, 65–80, 119–121
  spiral of, 51
  stress and, 13
  substance, 7
  support groups, 124
  symptoms, 7–8, 16–20
  urges in, 51
  withdrawal, 8, 122
adult chat rooms, 28–31, 51, 77
  anonymity in, 56
  cybersex, 29
  sexual fantasies, 29
Alcoholics Anonymous (AA), 77–78,
  152–153, 155
alcoholism, 11, 19, 147
anxiety, 73, 104–106
auctions, online, 43–45
Augustine, Saint, 54–55

bestiality, 28
bingeing, 11
blogging, 77
bondage, 28
Brody, Karen, 116

chat rooms. *See also* adult chat rooms
  anonymity in, 31–34
  false identities in, 34–36
child pornography. *See* pedophilia
children
  cyber pedophiles, 99, 111
  exposure to violence, 101, 111
  parents' ignorance of Internet
    activity, 97–98, 108–109
  pornography and, 100. *See also*
    pedophilia; pornography
  social anxiety and Internet
    addiction, 104–106
college students. *See under* Internet
compassion, 28
compulsive personalities, 76–77
confession. *See* reconciliation,
  sacrament of
Confessions (Augustine), 54
counseling
  twelve-step programs, 151–154, 160
  when to seek, 111, 150–151
Counter-Strike, 117–118
Created in God's Image (Koch), 31
cyberporn. *See* pornography
cybersex
  accidental exposure to, 53
  fantasy and, 28–29, 30
  sex addicts and, 78–80
  symptoms of addiction, 30
cybershakes, 122